Atonement for a 'Sinless' Society

'In spite of the centrality of the cross to biblical faith, old formulations and cultural formulations today cloud its significance. Alan Mann's voice is needed and welcome. In these pages, we find a moving narrative of atonement – from a penetrating analysis of the world we inhabit to the resolution of the human experience of chronic shame in the invitation of the Eucharist.'

Joel B. Green, Dean of Academic Affairs and Professor of New Testament Interpretation

'Thought-provoking, mission focused and culturally challenging … an insightful, timely and creative view of the atonement for our postmodern times.'

Steve Chalke, Founder Oasis Global and Faithworks

'A creative and well-researched presentation of faith thinking … anyone who desires to communicate the Gospel to a contemporary audience will find this both a challenging and a rewarding read.'

From the foreword by Graham McFarlane, Lecturer in Systematic Theology, London School of Theology

'Rather than simply repeating an articulation of the gospel from another time and culture, Alan Mann asks how the cross is good news for his culture and how to communicate that good news in his context today. We have much to learn from how he answers those questions.'

Mark D. Baker, Assistant Professor of Mission and Theology, Mennonite Brethren Biblical Seminary

'The first time I heard that devout and thoughtful Christians were questioning conventional understandings of atonement, I was shocked and concerned. As I explored further, I became convinced that this rethinking is essential, as Alan Mann's striking new book exemplifies. I found it clear, creative, deep, compelling, and inspiring.'

Brian McLaren, Pastor (crcc.org), Author (anewkindofchristian.com)

Atonement for a 'Sinless' Society
Engaging with an Emerging Culture

Alan Mann

PATERNOSTER

First published in 2005 by Paternoster Press,
Paternoster Press is an imprint of Authentic Media,
9 Holdom Avenue, Bletchley, Milton Keynes, Bucks,
MK1 1QR, UK
129 Mobilization Drive, Waynesboro, GA 30830-4575, USA
www.authenticmedia.co.uk/paternoster

British Library Cataloguing in Publication Data

A catalogue record for this book is available from the
British Library

ISBN 1-84227-355-8

Cover design by 4-9-0 ltd
Print Management by Adare Carwin
Printed and Bound by J. H. Haynes & Co. Ltd., Sparkford

Faith in an Emerging Culture Series Preface

Series Editor Pete Ward

It is common knowledge that Western culture has undergone major changes and we now find ourselves in an increasingly postmodern (or post-postmodern?), post Christendom, post industrial, post-just-about-anything-you-like world. The church now sits on the margins of western culture with a faith 'package deal' to offer the world that is perceived as out of date and irrelevant. How can we recontextualize the old, old story of the gospel in the new, new world of postmodernity? How can we fulfill our missional calling in a world that cannot any longer understand or relate to what we are saying? 'Faith in an Emerging Culture' seeks to imaginatively rethink Christian theology and practice in postmodern ways. It does not shrink from being explorative, provocative and controversial but is at the same time committed to remaining within the bounds of orthodox Christian faith and practice. Most readers will find things to agree with and things which will irritate them but we hope at very least to provoke fresh thought and theological/spiritual renewal.

For KAY

In this 'sinful' world your beauty
and goodness shine

Contents

Foreword   xi
Musings and Methodology   1

I   The Stories We Tell: Contemporary Perceptions
     about Sin and Shame   13
  1. A Narrative-Shift towards Innocence   15
  2. From Sin to Shame   31
  3. Shame and Atonement: Some Issues to Consider   46

II   The Function of Narrative: Story, Self and
     the Shape of Things to Come   61
  4. Narrative Now   63
  5. Narrative Possibilities   76
  6. Narrative and Christian Soteriology   90

III The Intent of Jesus in the Gospels:
     Atonement as Ontological Coherence   105
  7. Jesus Narrates His Intent: A Story of Coherence   107
  8. Judas and the Disciples: Narrative Incoherence   121
  9. From 'Death' to Life: The Hope of
     Ontological Coherence   132

IV Indwelling the Counter-Narrative:
     Rereading the Eucharist   147
10. A Rite of Identification   149
11. A Confrontation with Self   161
12. An Act of 'Communion'   172

The End of the Beginning:
Some Closing Thoughts   183
Let the Conversation Begin: A Response to
Alan Mann   188
We all know where we are coming from, but do
we know where we are going: A Response to
Robin Parry   199
Notes   211
Bibliography   220

Foreword

This book might be paraphrased, 'How does the story of Jesus' death touch base with the life stories of contemporary Westerners in a culture that no longer believes in the reality of sin?'.

It is widely recognized that Western culture is undergoing significant change. What is less recognized by many Christians is the fact that, at each previous cultural shift, the church has sought to re-articulate what it believes about the death of Jesus. This is, after all, the *thinking* and *communicating* role of the church. It is *why* we have theology in the first place. It is not surprising, then, that there is renewed need to communicate the death of Jesus in vibrant ways for this new, *post*modern, culture. What worked for the past three hundred to a thousand years may not be adequate today. There may be need for revision. This is exactly what Mann seeks to do in this book. The strength of his argument is that, at an *evangelistic* level, we need to first understand the place where sin impacts our contemporaries so that we can then address how the gospel can be 'Good News'. Whilst appeals to divine Law and God's holiness have been central to the modern era, they may not be the first port of

call for postmodern hearers. Thus, whilst not down-
grading the importance of particularly *modern* models of
the cross, Mann's desire is to make contact with where
his audience is today. In this sense, he stands in good
tradition, whether with the pastor seeking to connect
with his congregation, or with the great theologians of
the church from Calvin, Abelard, Anselm to Irenaeus.
Within the diversity of atonement models available
today, Mann wishes to offer one based on the concept of
shame as the point of contact with today's audience.

However, lest the reader think that *Atonement for a
Sinless Society* advocates postmodern relativism, the
argument soon turns from these cultural observations to
engagement with Scripture itself. Here Mann is his most
creative and seeks to cohere Jesus' story with today via a
presentation of Judas' story 'as a paradigm for the post-
industrialized storied-self'. With the biblical material
largely focused on the Passion Narratives, the argument
concludes with Mann presenting the Eucharist as the
point of contact from which the church may express its
own story and that of Jesus to postmodern hearers who
seek some kind of transcendental that will deal with their
sense of shame.

This is a creative and well-researched presentation of
faith thinking. It certainly does not fit neatly into one
particular box. It will challenge and possibly unnerve the
reader who holds to traditional or Reformed interpretations of the cross, and yet it will encourage such readers
to think through how their understanding of the cross
reaches out to postmodern audiences. It will empower
any evangelist who wrestles with the question of
communication. The reader from a high church position
will be encouraged by the emphasis on liturgy but
perhaps challenged by the evangelical zeal of the author.
Regardless of your theological position and tradition,

however, the problem of sin, which the cross seeks to resolve, is an important battleground in an increasingly secularized and therapeutic society. Therefore anyone who desires to communicate the gospel to a contemporary audience will find this both a challenging and a rewarding read. Mann presents the problem well and maps how our perception of the problem impacts the effectiveness of our communication of the solution. He takes the reader through various dialogues – narratives – to his own understanding of how the story of Jesus can become a liberating reality for the unchurched and churched alike.

Graham McFarlane,
Senior Lecturer in Systematic Theology,
London School of Theology

Musings and Methodologies

> ... we all hear them using our own languages to tell the wonderful things God has done. (Acts 2:11, CEV)

In her work *Speaking in Parables,* Sallie TeSelle posits the idea that 'the purpose of theology is to make it possible for the gospel to be heard in our time'.[1] Its relevancy, therefore, is dependent upon the theologian embracing the role of interpreter and standing in the gap between the often dissonant voices of the ancient and the (post)-modern. Consequently, the hermeneutical task for theologians is to create an atmosphere in which people feel comfortable using their own 'language' (and by this I mean language in all its fullness – symbolic, meta-phorical, etc.) to speak about theological, biblical and spiritual concerns, rather than relying on a 'language' that is unintelligible to them because of cultural distance and dissonance. If theologians themselves cannot actually translate the language of the gospel from one culture to another, then they should at least try to create an atmosphere in which others might feel at liberty to do so. This is an unenviable task in a post-industrialized context, where generations are no longer measured in scores of years but by the fingers of a single hand. However, we must not shy away from the challenge – not because TeSelle calls us to it, but because the one who the story is about does so. God issues this call implicitly, through incarnation, which takes seriously the need for atonement to be communicated in the context of human culture and language, and he calls explicitly in sending out his followers, then and now, into diverse environments.

Metaphorically and theologically, our post-industrialized, post-Christian, postmodern context needs a new *Pentecost*. Far too often, we speak a foreign language when we tell the story of atonement – not because the story itself is irrelevant, even to a 'sinless' society, but because we persist in thinking about it in narrow terms and in illustrating its significance in out-moded ways. Theologically, liturgically, culturally and philosophically the Christian community is so rich; and yet we live among the ruins of modernity as if we are paupers. As Joel B. Green and Mark Baker have pointed out, 'Many of us have been content merely to repeat the words of the New Testament itself, as though these words were themselves self-interpreting, requiring no translation'[2] – and this despite the fact that many within the worshipping community itself struggle to under-stand the purpose and wisdom of much of the language that pertains to the events of the passion of Christ. In reality, the question: What is the importance of the death of Jesus? 'typically attracts either no answers at all, other than looks of puzzlement, or endorsements of . . . "penal substitutionary atonement" [which many believe] in-terprets the significance of Jesus' death fully, completely, without remainder.'[3] This last observation is most tragic, for despite our confidence that *we* have the atonement pinned down, it remains anathema to the majority of people who we encounter within our towns and cities because we insist on speaking a language that was once fruitful but is now incomprehensible. To postmodern sensibilities, the crucifixion of Jesus was nothing more than a primitive, barbaric, pointless death.

At Pentecost, the people gathered were 'surprised' to hear Jesus' followers communicating to them in their own language and, as a result, they became a captive audience, willing to listen because they were able to understand. In the same way, the Christian community needs to 'surprise' its contemporaries by telling the story of atonement in the language of the postmodern and so captivate them, in many cases for the first time, with a meaningful and sufficient account of the Passion Narrative.

Daunting and dubious as this may sound to some, a glance over the pages of the history of atonement theory soon reveals a reactive tradition to the needs of any given peoples. Therefore, the gospel narrative should not become a museum piece, and neither should the theology and cultural awareness that we derive from them. We need to read and reread the atonement as time and place change the context in which we are called to communicate the salvific work of Christ. Our responsibility, as it has been since the paradigmatic intervention of the incarnation, is to discern the overarching predicament of our time, to understand *the* question behind the questions of our cultural and philosophical context, and to engage them with a meaningful and sufficient story of atonement. Each new frontier of Christian mission requires fresh theological pursuit. We are not called to rest on our laurels, to speak of, discuss and implement the theologies of our forebears as if they are determinative for all contexts everywhere. Rather, we are to be a community out of which ever-new expressions of our faith can emerge. This is a wonderfully creative process, but it is also a risky one. For 'the problem with atonement theologies is that they are sometimes so perceptive and brilliant that they last beyond their appropriate time – and, at the same time, they are perpetuated longer than should be because too few Christians have the courage to enter into the new, emerging darkness and prefer to rely on the old light of entrenched soteriologies'.[4]

This, of course, leads simply to the following questions. What is our time? How do postmodern, post-industrialized, post-Christian people see themselves? And what influence will that have on the theological task of making the gospel heard? These are huge questions with myriad answers, but they are also the questions of culture and context that the church has always faced. Indeed, they are the questions answered by incarnation.

The starting point for what follows is the desire to wrestle with the observation that we increasingly live in a 'sinless' society. That is, individuals no longer live with a sense of sin or guilt in the way that evangelists would wish them to in order to successfully communicate the atoning work of Christ. If this can be proved a true observation, then the implications for the Christian community and its models of atonement are obvious. Though evangelistic initiatives may wish to chart a society in which sin still abounds, the increasing reality is that the plight of individuals in the post-industrialized West is that they are, 'a sinner with no word for it'.[5]

There is a measurable hermeneutical task here. This task involves dealing with worldview questions. What's wrong? What's the solution? It is a task that deals with the limitations of a culture, a deficit in its understanding – and it does so by approaching that deficit through observing the rise of, and appropriating, the implications of narrative for self-understanding. Therefore, of utmost importance are questions regarding the role of the reader, the psychological self, the storied-self: what do they bring to the narratives of atonement, what do they look for, what do they understand?

There is a slight irony in the fact that the decision to approach this issue via the use of narrative has subconsciously shaped the work itself. The following chapters take the form of a narrative structure, moving from a place of conflict to resolution (What's wrong? What's the solution?).

The opening chapter establishes the conflict. Drawing on cultural commentary, psychotherapy and examples from popular film and literature, Chapter 1 charts the demise of sin and guilt in the storytelling vocabulary of many living in the post-industrialized West. We will see that the stories we tell seldom, if ever, attribute sin, guilt or wrongness to ourselves. In turn, geneticists, sociologists and psychologists increasingly legitimize our narratives and allow us to live in the confidence that we do no wrong. From the cult of victim to the loss of moral categories, the chapter also discusses the loss of the 'Other' (historically, socially and spiritually) and its role in extinguishing the embers of sin and guilt.

The claim of Chapter 2 is that while the postmodern self is able to push away sin and guilt in relation to 'Others', the intensity of the emphasis upon self has created an often-crippling phenomenon, typically labelled shame. Shame, or our failure to live to an ideal that we have held for ourselves, is an experience of self-deficiency. What the postmodern craves, therefore, is an ontological coherence – a wholeness of being that always seems to be out of reach. The fallout from this is far-reaching, but perhaps of most significance for the individual is the social isolation that ensues, which drives an irreconcilable search for intimacy due to the fact that the subject of that search is only ever 'I'.

The final chapter of the first section of the book considers the implications of all of the above for the Christian church and its central desire to communicate the atoning work of Christ to a lost world. As we shall see, the problem is relatively easy to establish, the solution a much more difficult prospect. Here the impasse will be spelled out in its starkest form: with sin and guilt there is at least the possibility of telling our story and relating our wrongdoing, bringing the possibility of forgiveness and reconciliation. With shame, the primary victim is the self, making intentional acts of confession an anathema.

The second section, 'The Function of Narrative: Story, Self and the Shape of Things to Come', develops the discussion about the importance of narrative both in shaping the individual and in the theological task in general. Therefore, Chapter 4 shows that, far from being a peripheral in our perceptions about ourselves and the world, story is now seen very much as a pervasive, necessary and constructive epistemological category. Sociologists, psychologists, theologians and, to an increasing degree, scientists are recognizing this and using narrative in their work. However, narrative is not without its difficulties in a postmodern world. Postmodern narratives are typically isolated, localized, personalized and pluralistic.

Chapter 5 focuses on the heart of the matter, discussing the possibility for, and the reality of, narrative constructing, deconstructing and then reconstructing the self. In considering the relatively new field of narrative therapy, we shall encounter the reality that the stories we actually tell are often ones of torment. Indeed, in the case of shame, they become cover stories to throw others off our scent; to protect us from the fear that our real-self may be exposed and that we will be despised. Because we are isolated by our stories and not liberated by them, narrative therapists have reached the conclusion that their role is to unlock this destructive cycle via counter-stories. Rather than dominating the analysand, however, the therapist works together with the patient to co-author a new story that can be inhabited. What the therapeutic community is doing explicitly is taking place implicitly on a day-to-day basis in the lives of every individual within the towns and cities of Western Europe. Via the media of film, television, novels, magazines, radio, internet, advertising and personal encounter, stories are told, retold, agreed with, countered and subverted. All of these storied events are an invitation to live as if the world they represent is the real world, even if that suggested reality counters and contrasts with the individual's current experience.

Chapter 6, 'Narrative and Christian Soteriology', takes this idea of the counter-narrative and simply suggests that conversion is, at one level, embracing an alternative story by which the person narrates his or her self. A storied approach to the atonement, therefore, as opposed to declaring it as a truthful proposition, is more likely to engage the postmodern with its meaning. This is because, firstly, it comes to them in a recognizable and less threatening manner and, secondly, because it professes to do no more than other narratives that are heard via therapy, novel, film or cyberspace – to live in the world they create as if it is the real world. Christian soteriology becomes the joining of the individual's story with the story of the Christian community and, by implication, with the story of God.

At this point the third section of the book, 'The Intent of Jesus in the Gospels: Atonement as Ontological Coherence', introduces us to the story of atonement as told through the Passion Narratives. Taking the narrative time frame between the Last Supper and the crucifixion, we read it in the light of the discussion thus far, taking into account the plight of the postmodern sinless self and the importance of narrative to that self in understanding their need of atonement.

In Chapter 7, we enter the story of atonement as Jesus and his disciples prepare to share what has become known as the Lord's, or the Last, Supper. However, to make it clear that it is the whole life of Jesus that is his work of atonement, with the cross its most potent symbol, relevant excursions will be made into the fuller account of the story. This chapter will argue that Jesus is an individual who narrates his identity and his intent to himself and to 'Others'. This is no more evident than around the table he shares with his friends on the eve of his execution. For the postmodern reader, the narrative tension soon becomes clear. For what Jesus is portraying is effectively his ideal-self. The question that arises, and which is played out in the events to come, is whether this Jesus is able to do precisely what the post-industrialized self knows he or she cannot do: namely, to coherently hold together the ideal- and the real-self. This is funda-mental in constructing a model of atonement for the post-industrialized sinless self, for without the intent of Jesus the cross itself becomes nothing more than a hollow act. The reader is looking for the hope of ontological co-herence, for the possibility of living free from shame. The self is seeking a narrative identity, which can hold together the ideal-/real-self without contradiction. Here, it will be argued, they can find such a story.

Running counter to Jesus' story is the intent of another – Judas. Therefore, in Chapter 8 we take a risk in turning to Judas' story as a paradigm for the post-industrialized storied-self, lost within a narrative that has lost its coherence. This is, after all, the despised betrayer of history. However, when Judas' story is handled in a more sympathetic way the reader becomes acquainted with one who is self-despising long before others despise him. Here is one who, like the postmodern, lacks the coherence he craves. Judas is also a victim in this story. He is the self-betrayed as much as he is the betrayer. Judas can easily be read as one whose life has become meaningless. His personal narrative has become unintelligible to him, lacking any point or movement towards resolution and ending in the ultimate complaint – the taking of his own life. But Judas isn't the only one lacking coherence, nor is he the only one doing the betraying. The other disciples demonstrate, one at a time, that they also all lack a consistency between intent and action, the ideal and the real-self. But, more than that, the power of the story is such that the reader cannot avoid repeating the anguished question raised by the disciples: 'Am I the betrayer?'

Chapter 8 ends with the suggestion that there is hope to be found in this narrative. Our betrayals are not deliberate acts but ontological failings. Just as the disciples are not against Jesus but are simply failing at being for him, so for the post-industrialized self: we are not against those with whom we seek intimacy. But this only remains a vain hope without the death and resurrection of Jesus. Chapter 9, therefore, argues that the cross is not a declaration by Jesus that the narrative of his life has collapsed and become unintelligible to him – it is a self-giving, not a hopeless giving up. Neither is it to be seen as the ultimate shaming of Jesus, a place to which no postmodern would be convinced that they should follow him. The cross, rather, is the public reality of the private symbolism of the Upper Room. The bread broken at the Lord's Supper is now brutally present on a hill named Golgotha. But it has to be so, for narration of intent without significant action leaves all concerned without the hope of liberation. Jesus' death takes place without contradiction and in the trust that God is able to continue to narrate his story beyond death.

Finally, the fourth section, 'Indwelling the Counter-story', finds a home for encountering and appropriating these narratives of atonement in the form of the Christian communities' continual re-enactment of them in the Eucharist.

In the first chapter of this final section of the book, Chapter 10, the argument is put forward that the Eucharist is a rite of identification, which allows for the atoning work of Jesus to manifest itself in the lives of those who encounter it. It is that moment when the death of the self can occur and the possibility of divine author-ship can become a real possibility. As the Eucharist is played out and the narrative of Jesus' intent, betrayal, forgiveness and eventual self-oblation is realized, the rite of identification calls on those present to offer and reorientate their lives in a similar way.

Chapter 11 suggests that the liturgy surrounding the Eucharist places words into our mouths to enable us to confess. This is not to dominate us, or to take us to a place that we do not wish to go, but to give us a point of recognition and to enable the self to move beyond the inadequacies of its own narrative. Through confession we are brought to awareness that there is an absence of the 'Other' in right relationship to us, including the absence of God. It is these arguments that allow us to talk of the place of atonement in a sinless society. The Eucharist, in this context, becomes a place for the post-industrialized self, isolated by shame, to discover for the first time transcendence and Otherness, to be atoned for, to be reconciled and to be authored once more by the creator of life.

Finally, we ask a vital question: where does the 'telling' take place? To the isolated individual, wrestling with the issue of their shame, the fact that the Eucharist has, indeed is, a communal activity, and not simply a rite of identification acted out in isolation, is vital. As Jesus faced the challenge of Gethsemane (the fear of failing in his resolve to go to the cross), so now also individuals must face their own dying to self, for they too are called to deny their self-seeking and self-justification and embrace the 'Other' in an act of mutual forgiveness. The community of faith is defined as a place of inclusion where the self is called to confess their old self and embrace their new identity so that they can be atoned for and reconciliation can occur.

While writing the manuscript for this book, the desire to qualify much that is suggested here, mainly to pre-empt inevitable criticism, was a constant companion. However, in the end I allowed myself to be comforted by the knowledge that even the most conservative and orthodox view of the atonement has its critics. It would seem that the truism 'you can't please all the people all of the time' was written for the Christian community. More than that, I did not wish the argument here to be lost in a fog of qualification, making the book a tedious read and rendering its potential impact impotent.

Though it engages with pastoral, psychological, philosophical and cultural concerns, ultimately this book is about a theology of atonement. What follows, however, will not be an easy read for the theologically faint-hearted. Indeed, at times it will appear utterly un-orthodox (but then, orthodoxy is never a useful term when dealing with the ephemeral nature of culture). In reality, however, the more astute reader will recognize that what takes place here has far more continuity than discontinuity with orthodox Christian belief, and that what appears radical is in fact nothing more than ortho-doxy in contemporary form.

J. Bowker once wrote, 'Theories of atonement are somewhat like lymphocytes in the body: they are solutions going around looking for a problem, and taking the shape of the problem as it is identified.'[6] The task we are faced with, therefore, is not to go on a crusade in order to search out the sin that has hidden itself among the ruins of modernity – for sin, as we shall see, has become meaningless and insufficient as a descriptor for the plight of the postmodern self. Stories define who we are, and counter-stories change who we are, if we will let them. Therefore the church needs to incarnate (or speak meaningfully) the story of atonement into a postmodern context so the story can be heard and understood and so bring about atonement. Although it is ultimately God, through the Holy Spirit, who reconciles us to himself, we need to play a part in communicating the story successfully.

I

The Stories We Tell

Contemporary Perceptions
about Sin and Shame

1. A Narrative-Shift towards Innocence

Sin doesn't really exist as a serious idea in modern life.[7]

For those who recognize the centrality of sin in the Christian story, which speaks of the plight of humanity and the saving actions of God in Christ upon the cross of Calvary, it is all too easy to become defensive when faced with the suggestion that sin does not really exist as a serious idea anymore. Sin, we may wish to argue, is a matter of fact not of opinion. The revelation of God to humanity is that 'all have sinned and fall short of the glory of God,' (Romans 3:23). This is the unquestionable reality we are faced with as we read the Scriptures and, it is argued, must be presented as such even to a society who are unwilling to entertain the idea of their sinfulness. To respond to Bryan Appleyard's statement simply by restating the bare facts is, however, to miss the thrust of the argument and even potentially jeopardize the ongoing missional work of the church in communicating the relevance of the atoning life of Jesus to an increasingly 'sinless' society. For what is driving this observation is not an issue of theology or indeed ontology, but the vehicle by which such things are communicated: language.

The working vocabulary of our culture has either dropped sin altogether as a description of our actions or it has shifted its semantic domain. That is, the force of its meaning has changed. This is not an uncommon phenomenon in the human construct we call language. Words and their meanings change, even from generation to generation. For example, few people today would express their emotional well-being as 'gay', for this word has shifted meaning. Semantics (the meaning of words and how they can change in time and context) is one of the fundamentals of biblical hermeneutics. If we ignore this phenomenon, then understanding and communication become perilous occupations.

One of the problems facing the church, and the issue at hand here, is that the word 'sin' has become just as tainted, polluted and defiled in the postmodern mind as the word itself indicates. Gone are the sins of the Protestant Reformation and the prudish psyche of our Victorian ancestors. Instead, the idea of sin, if it is used at all, has to a large extent simply been absorbed into the consumerist and entertainment culture that is so prevalent in the developed nations of the West. Sin has been caricatured, a tool for advertisers to suggest that a product is good and pleasurable. Far from being something to be avoided, sin is now part and parcel of the human desire that drives consumerist mentalities. As Appleyard himself goes on to say, 'We take sin seriously [only] as a way of making life more exciting. We want to keep the sins [and by this he means the seven deadly kind], but only so we can have fun committing them. The idea that such acts may be insults to God, to the fabric of the world, seems to be lost forever.'[8]

Again, a Christian response to this statement may be to point to the implicit hedonistic debauchery implied by such ideas that indicate categorically the reality that sin is alive and well in our society. However, a knee-jerk response may cause us to gloss over the fact that we are being told a dimension of the important story, 'What it means to be a person living in a post-industrialized, post-Christian society'. We must listen to this story, hearing it in all its complexity, if we are to communicate success-fully the atoning work of Jesus. We ignore the power of stories at our peril. Indeed, if we ignore them we actually misunderstand ourselves as Christians, for we too are people of a story. We 'narrate' ourselves in light of the biblical story and the church community of which we are a part. To be Christian is to tell a story that holds meaning for us. Our dilemma, however, is that this story is all too often retold in such a way that it has no meaning for others. And that is precisely the quandary we have when it comes to sin and atonement. Society and contemporary culture are reflecting back to us the story they hear and the meaning (or lack of it) it has for them. Not-withstanding the church's insistence on the validity and truth of the content, it is a story that has lost all sense and significance for individuals because they are, to all intents and purposes, 'sinless'.

If we listen attentively to the stories being told by those outside the church, what we will hear reflected back to us, time and again, is the idea that sin is understood solely as an offence against a divinely instituted law – because this is the only story people hear from the church itself: we are bad people because we *do* bad things. In some senses this is a biblical understanding of what sin is – though a highly simplified version. However, as we shall discuss further, such an understanding requires an acute sense of 'Other', which is often lacking in the mindset of the vast majority who live largely autonomous lives – socially, spiritually and morally. Once transcendence, represented by the 'Other', is gone, then the credibility of a narrative that relies on it to define actions as wrong (or good) is severely undermined. You are then left in precisely the place we find ourselves, in a world in which the word 'sin' no longer means what the evangelists wish it to. When the church seeks to speak to the society around it about sin and atonement, people hear amiss. There is a clash of narratives, and the one that makes the most sense to the hearer will be the one that will win out.

The post-industrialized self perceives him or herself to be innocent because of the narrative-shift in the stories they tell. We can trace myriad and complex reasons for this shift,[9] and we shall consider some of these below, if only briefly. At this early stage, however, it is worth bringing to the forefront of our minds the not uncommon understanding of sin that drives our stories of atonement.

Professor Douglas John Hall, in his work *The Cross in Our Context*, cuts to the heart of the problem when he writes:

> No word in the Christian vocabulary is so badly understood both in the world and in the churches as the word sin. Christians have allowed this profoundly biblical conception, which refers to broken relationships, to be reduced to sins – moral misdemeanors and guilty "thoughts, words, and deeds," especially of the sexual variety, that could be listed and confessed and absolved.[10]

This poor, or reductionist, understanding of sin is at least partly responsible for the decline of Christianity in the West precisely because it has sought to quantify something that is first and foremost about the *quality* of our relationships with each other, the world we live in and the God who created it. As Hall further states, 'The result is a petty moralism that no longer speaks to … human persons in their complex intermingling.'[11] Sin has rather unhelpfully been reduced solely to the *presence* of wrongful actions when in reality (as the thrust of the argument here will show) it would have far greater meaning for individuals living in our post-industrialized society to describe it as an *absence* of mutual, intimate, undistorted relating that ultimately leads the post-modern self into a lack of ontological (or narrative) coherence (all will become clear later).

Having stated this working definition of sin, the purpose of what follows will not be to advocate the conservative option of preaching the sinfulness of human-kind in the vain hope that people will come, hear and respond to such a message. As should be clear by now, the assumption, based on the observations above and below, is that sin, while certainly not a meaningless word, is one that is so misunderstood and misused that it is rendered almost useless as a descriptor of the needs and inadequacies of individuals in relating to 'Others'. Rather, we will seek to listen carefully to the story of the post-industrialized self and to draw from the deep well that is a biblical understanding of sin as an issue of relational ontology, and so engage the self with narratives that will speak meaningfully to their predicament and give fresh insight into the atoning work of Jesus. For, as we saw in the introduction above, the nature of the biblical narratives about atonement and the historical theories that followed give us the mandate to contextualize the saving work of Christ for the time and place in which we find ourselves – in our case, the context of a post-industrialized, post-Christian, 'sinless' society'.

Sin and the absence of the 'Other'

One of the key factors in generating a 'sinless' society is the increasing absence of the 'Other' in contemporary perceptions about the self. This absence is observable, to a greater or lesser degree, at the social level of the neighbour and at the spiritual level of the divine, defined as the giver of moral imperatives. For while it is true that the postmodern pursues spirituality with some vigour, it is seldom expressed in terms of a relationship with a personal being. Far more common is the idea of a personally constructed spirituality, a tailor-made way of being that fits current needs or desires in the hope of generating a sense of calm and well-being for the 'inner-self' in a form of pseudo-Buddhism that reaches within for truth, moral awareness and wholeness. With such a privately structured spirituality, where any god that may exist is only thought about in deist terms, there is little if anything to sin against except one's self. There is no god to judge our actions, only our own sense of morality, our personal ideal – our own personal story. The only rewards or consequences for our actions are self-generating. All the postmodern is sure about is that he or she is alive now. There is only this life. 'Heaven' or 'hell' is purely dependent on the success or failure of *'project self'* – life here and now is either heaven or hell.

The roots of this autonomy and subsequent absence of the 'Other' have been traced, time and again, to the cultural, scientific and religious paradigm shift that was the Enlightenment. Yet it is perhaps its cultural and philosophical cousin, Romanticism, that is the true ancestor of the postmodern. For while the search goes on within for 'moral and spiritual truths', these increasingly remain true only for the self, finding only coincidental expression beyond the self.

> The postmodern is in every way a child of the romantics …
> The difference is that the postmodern self no longer
> harbours hopes of discovering truth or secure principles
> [defined universally]. Instead, driven by the ideals of
> therapy and consumption, it seeks … to provide satisfac-
> tions for the unencumbered self; it strives to reduce all
> individual moral actions to matters of choice for which
> there are no authoritative guidelines or binding principles.
> In the culture of therapy and interpretation, there is nothing
> to direct the self except its preferences. There is no goal for
> the actions of the self save the fulfilment of its desires.[12]

Based on Lundin's observations, Middleton and Walsh
suggest that choice 'becomes not an owning of responsibility but an escape from allowing oneself to be held
accountable'.[13] Indeed, in our post-industrialized
societies moral ambiguity can even be seen as a
judgement-free human right, where 'an increasing
number of individuals actually defend infidelity and betrayal as the prerogatives of authentic selfhood'.[14]

If 'sin' exists at all, we encounter it only when we fail
to devote ourselves to the project of self-realization. Even
the briefest of glances over the 'Mind, Body, Spirit' or
'Popular Psychology' sections of a high-street book shop
leaves you in no doubt that the pursuit of self-awareness,
self-esteem, wholeness and well-being is paramount. To
be *self-centred* is a twenty-first century virtue, for no
'Other' can be trusted to bring the 'good life' craved by
the postmodern. One who fails at 'project self' (a failure
defined by the individual's own ideas of success based
upon cultural and social influences) must gaze into the
mirror and confess: 'Against you alone have I sinned.'

Of course, it could easily be argued that the Christian
narrative encompasses what should be seen as the 'sin' of
pride. Indeed, pride is perhaps the 'original' sin that led

to the fall. But this is not strictly so when we take a post-industrialized society as our context. For Adam and Eve, so the story tells us, rebelled against a God they knew intimately. Such intimacy is not part of the story the post-modern tells, especially in relation to the divine. In our cultural context, 'What is called pride … is generally a cover-up for deep-seated *dis-ease* with oneself.'[15] This pride should be pitied, not judged, for there is no viable option for the self living in a world without trans-cendence. This is not the kind of rebellion that led to the fall, but a clinging to all that is left when the 'Other' no longer plays a significant part in the story: 'What it means to be human.'

The absence of the 'Other' and the resulting self-centredness also have the effect of detaching the self from any historical construction of identity. The irony of Lundin's claim that Romanticism is the ancestor of the postmodern is that, to a large extent, the postmodern rejects the very idea of being defined by such historical constructs because the past is, quite literally, an absent 'Other'. There is little space made for metanarrative, the overarching story that tells of who we are, where we have come from, what is wrong with our world and where we are heading (something we will return to in Part II). The postmodern will reject the traditional ways of narrating the self (such as those of the major world faiths), perceiving that they rely on metanarrative for their construction of the self. If there is no 'Other' then there is no past, no tradition to define us and, more importantly, no future to be defined, no peoples for whom to leave a tradition. Everything is collapsed into the fleeting reality of the present.

> [P]retending to be embryos, pretending to be like foetuses … Our minds would be blank and our eyes closed as we

floated in warm waters ... isolated in our foetal stupor we would bump into each other in the deep end, like twins with whom we didn't even know we shared a womb ... Ours was a life lived in paradise and thus rendered any discussion of transcendental ideas pointless. Politics, we supposed, existed elsewhere in a televised non-paradise; death was something similar to recycling. Life was charmed but without politics or religion. It was the life of children of the children of the pioneers – life after God – a life of earthly salvation on the edge of heaven.[16]

Coupland's 'fictional' observation about our post-industrialized context gives popular credence to the idea that '[s]ince "the society" has no future, it makes sense to live only for the moment, to fix our eyes on our own "private performance," to become connoisseurs of our own decadence, to cultivate a "transcendental self-attention."'[17] Life after God so easily becomes life without the 'Other' in so many ways. Transcendence is, quite literally, beyond the narrative of much of the post-industrialized self. We have developed into 'a self-indulgent society in which the disciplines of neighborliness, that is the attention to the other, have disappeared'.[18] We live in a 'sinless' society because without the 'Other' there are no subjects to have wronged. And this means that language of repentance has little purpose or meaning either. In the narrative of the post-industrialized self, if there is something wrong with the world that requires blame, or responsibility, then the problem must lie elsewhere – not with the self.

As the post-industrialized self sheds its belief in, and reliance on, history and metanarrative, so the trust of institutions collapses also – for institutions are, by and large, the products of that same history and the carriers of the metanarratives that perpetuate doubted truth into the present. The much-bemoaned incredulity towards the church as an institution is not so much a personal attack on our particular brand of truth, or on the story we have to share, as it is merely part of a wider cultural shift, affecting all our institutions. Whereas some institutions find it difficult to discover a friendly ear for their political ideologies or sociological theories, the church struggles to find sympathy for its stories about God, humankind and the fate of the created order. As the writer and activist Kay Carmichael observes, 'Ever since the 1960s [the seedbed of much we now call postmodern], the authority of the church in matters of morality has been steadily diminishing. [So much so that even its own members] have increasingly been creating their own definitions of what is and is not sinful behaviour.'[19]

Growing alongside the saplings of postmodernity, a secular morality emerged based upon rights rather than responsibilities. In a chapter rather aptly named 'How to be Sinless', the church historian Meic Pearse fleshes out the rise of human rights and how they came to dominate 'our concepts of right and wrong and of permissibility and impermissibility',[20] particularly in the late twentieth century. Detailed as his argument is, there are simple yet important observations to be made from Pearse's work. Most notable is the narrative-shift in responsibility away from the individual and on to 'an amorphous, impersonal "them" … [who] are to blame for everything.'[21]

If only psychologically, human rights free us from human wrong. In the story that the post-industrialized self tells, obligations and responsibilities for public well-being lie fairly and squarely with institutions. We no longer give to the poor because we expect financial support to be given and provision to be made. The obligation lies with institutions, not the individual. And 'if we have no obligations, then there are no duties that I have failed to fulfil, no forbidden acts that I should feel guilty about having done. I cannot envisage myself as a sinner, not even before a Holy God.'[22] As the institutions fail us, however, *they* can perhaps be said to have sinned, giving rise to the irony that the institution of the church, which should hold narratives of liberation for the postmodern, is in fact perceived to be an oppressor who 'sins against us'.

There is fruitful work being done on the issue of 'structural sin', of how institutions are perhaps seen as the harbourers of sin in a post-industrialized context and how the cross might speak into this situation. In many ways, however, this only goes to affirm the postmodern story that the individual is without responsibility or obligation and is, more importantly, an 'innocent victim' when the language of sin is employed.

Victimization and our therapeutic liberation from sin and guilt

At the heart of many contemporary stories lies the afore-mentioned victim. The implication is that we are more *sinned against* than sinner. As the victim we are helpless, the casualty of social structures, institutions and corporate bodies. It is with them that responsibility lies, not with the 'innocent victim' of their distorted practices. As the distinguished journalist John Humphrys wrote as he reflected on our current moral, social and cultural context, 'If you are a victim it is because someone or something is to *blame* for the predicament you find yourself in.'[23] Even the therapist, when employed to bring meaning into our dysfunctional lives, seldom encourages clients to look beyond themselves, to the interests of others or the responsibilities and obligations they may have towards them. Nor do therapists direct clients to institutions that might carry narratives of hope and liberation from their *dis-ease*. Indeed 'in personal counselling, practitioners make it a point of professional honor never to express moral judgements, so the word "fault" – let alone the word "sin" – will never pass their lips.'[24] That is because the only obligation the client has is to his or her own self-realization, something deemed achievable without the 'Other', who is more likely to be perceived as the cause of our traumas rather than the answer to them.

'It's not your fault' has become a theme that holds much kudos in the way we tell the contemporary story of human responsibility. Robin William's martyr-like therapist in the film *Good Will Hunting* perfectly portrays this point in cinematic form.[25] Though the immediate context might possibly have warranted it, the forceful repetition of the phrase 'It's not your fault' during one scene towards the end of the film only serves to emphasize who the victim is, despite Will Hunting's obvious failings. And, as the victim, Will Hunting gains our sympathy and not our judgement. That's because, by convincingly playing the role of the victim, we cloud the vision of those around us so it is more difficult for them to see how we victimize others. In the therapeutic culture of Western society in the twenty-first century, 'whoever can claim the status of victim with greater authority wins, because that status projects an image of innocence over against which all others are somehow guilty'.[26] Our society neither sees as beneficial nor encourages the individual to recognize and accept that we all succumb to the temptation to victimize others. Indeed, the position of victim, the position of weakness, is in fact a position of power for social and political manoeuvring, and so we wish to perpetuate the truth or illusion that we are the victim because 'claiming the exclusive status of a victim carries with it an invitation … to the power that comes with remaining immersed in the stories of one's own – or one's people's own – victimization.'[27]

This idea of the power of the victim has even found its way into the popular theology of the church, with Jesus playing the role of the ultimate victim – an innocent at the hands of powerful religious and political structures. To illustrate this perfectly one only has to tease out the elements of a favoured 'preacher's parable' known as 'The Long Silence'. A crowd of billions gathers on a great plain at the end of time. There they wait, before God's throne of judgement. But while most are portrayed as cowering at the thought of what awaits them, a belligerent group towards the front decides to question God's right to judge them. So it is that a 'delegation of suffering' is sent to confront God and put his credentials to the test:

> Before God could be qualified to be their judge, He must endure what they had endured. Their decision was that God should be sentenced to live on earth as a man.
>
> Let him be born a Jew. Let the legitimacy of his birth be doubted. Give him a work so difficult that even his family will think him out of his mind.
>
> Let him be betrayed by his closest friends. Let him face false charges, be tried by a prejudiced jury and convicted by a cowardly judge. Let him be tortured.
>
> At the last, let him see what it means to be terribly alone. Then let him die so there can be no doubt he died. Let there be a great host of witnesses to verify it.
>
> As each leader announced his portion of the sentence, loud murmurs of approval went up from the throng of people

assembled. When the last had finished pronouncing sentence, there was a long silence. No one uttered a word. No one moved.

For suddenly, all knew that God had already served His sentence.

The 'victims' are left dumbfounded – not by God's holiness, but by his status as the ultimate victim. And so all the other victims wait to be judged by God for, as everyone knows, the ultimate victim wins.

While this wonderfully contrived piece of theatre preaches well, its appropriateness in a victim-based culture must be questioned. As Joel Green and Mark Baker have already suggested, 'Locating Jesus, characterized as the willing victim of unjust suffering, at the heart of Christian faith is for some tantamount to idealizing the values of the victim and advising the abused to participate in their own victimization.'[28] With so many willing victims living among us, how helpful can it be to place power in the hands of the ultimate victim, to generate a narrative around the cross of Christ and justify God as judge on the basis that Jesus suffered the most? Surely the narratives we build around the atonement should be replete with the possibility that such victim-mentalities (and realities) have been significantly dealt with by the cross, and we should not help to perpetuate the common idea that being the victim can serve to furnish our lives with a social defence mechanism?

Instead of owning responsibility and allowing sin and guilt to be laid at his or her feet, the post-industrialized self lives as a moral centrifuge, spinning on the axes of scientific, social and therapeutic justification. Responsibility is thrown off into 'prior causes … such things as childhood trauma, unconscious conflict, or bio-chemistry'.[29] Psychologists search for the trauma that has shaped our dysfunctional self, beginning almost from the moment the zygote of our existence was formed. Influenced by psychological and sociological theory, academics offer to us their theories about the effects on behaviour of poverty, parental abuse and environmental factors. These external forces are to be held responsible, not the 'innocent' individual. Even the societies in which we live find it increasingly difficult to charge the individual with moral misdemeanour, opting instead to excuse each other, unsure of the boundaries or matrices by which social relations should be determined.

Geneticists and their counterparts chart the human genome, convinced that they can simply switch off our propensity to wrong others, an excess of grey matter in the brain's frontal lobe justification for a criminal mentality. 'Science [has] led directly to the idea that sinning may not be the sinner's fault. ... The idea of a free choice to sin [has been] compromised ... with the advent of modern genetics ... the possibility [has] emerged that nobody [can] ever be said to be guilty ... because nobody has a free choice to do anything.'[30] What residue of sin that may remain in us, what responsibility and obligation we have failed to shake off onto meaningless meta-narratives, oppressive institutions and impersonal systems, can at last be put down to the fact that ultimately we are the victim of our own genetic make-up.

It would seem that we move ever closer to a society free from personal guilt, free from the traditional religious language of sin. In their person-centred narratives, postmoderns become victims of the world. Indeed we have even become victims of ourselves. We seek not salvation – as defined in a religious manner – but liberation, as defined psychologically, 'the feeling, the momentary illusion, of personal well-being, health and psychic security'.[31] The question still remains, however: Has the the postmodern self truly found its liberation in the narratives it has produced – narratives free from sin and responsibility towards the 'Other'? Is a 'sinless' society a utopia in no need of atonement, or is 'sin' (as defined above) simply hidden in the vocabulary the post-industrialized self uses to tell the story 'What it means to be a person living in a post-industrialized, post-Christian society'?

2. From Sin to Shame

Now that I have eyes for it, I see [shame] everywhere.[32]

While the post-industrialized self is able to push away the sins of moral misdemeanour (for all the reasons set out in the previous chapter), the intensity of the emphasis placed upon the self has generated a chronic, internalized *dis-ease*, typically labelled 'shame'. Shame, however, is not an easy concept to pin down. It is a complex and at times contradictory phenomenon. It is pervasive and virulent, destroying the very basis of mutual, intimate, undistorted relating, and it cries out to be recognized and addressed if Christian communities are to be known as places of healing, restoration and reconciliation for the post-industrialized self.

Perhaps it needs to be stated early on that we are all vulnerable to shame because we are human. Indeed, the success of books such as John Bradshaw's *Healing the Shame that Binds You,*[33] which has sold well in excess of half a million copies, only serves to emphasize the self-awareness many have regarding this uniquely personal experience. Shame has so consumed some, however, that they have taken on the identity of a shamed person and can only relate to themselves and to others as such.

One of the most powerful descriptions of the horror that is shame comes from the pen of Gershen Kaufman: 'Shame is felt as an inner torment, a sickness of the soul', he writes. 'It is the most poignant experience of the self by the self … a wound from the inside, dividing us both from ourselves and from one another.'[34] Equally it has been described as 'internalised pollution', a staining, defiling *dis-ease* rendering the sufferer worthless in his or her own sight, 'dehumanising to the extent that it changes the person into excrement – something low, stained, unpleasant, and unwanted in their own eyes.'[35] These are helpful descriptors to keep at the forefront of our minds when seeking to speak meaningfully about atonement to a 'sinless' society. Yet it is the voices of those who suffer from shame that should cause us to pause and listen to the stories of the 'sinless' and think afresh about the atonement as a means of healing the relational self.

> 'My self feels diminished'
> 'A feeling of being dirty, defiled, unwanted'
> 'Feeling demeaned and put on view'
> 'There is nowhere to hide'
> 'A feeling of exposure'
> 'Being wrong without knowing why'
> 'Not being good enough'[36]

As these brief quotes show, by its very nature shame is a complex, multidimensional and multi-layered condition. Common to all of these stories, however, is the theme of self-judgement. The chronically shamed person holds a fervent belief that he or she is utterly deficient as a human being, incapable of maintaining his or her own self-coherence and inner-relatedness, let alone being of sufficient social ability and worth to relate to others without dysfunction. There is a fundamental tension in the story postmoderns tell. They constantly live with the possibility of a total and utter collapse in their personal narrative. And if a person's narrative collapses, then the self is in danger of disintegrating. For as human beings we exist – psychologically, socially and spiritually – through the stories we tell about ourselves. We will discuss these ideas at length in Part II. For the moment, bold as it may be, it will be sufficient to suggest from this observation that if our post-industrialized societies are going to have a future, then the issue of personal shame needs to be acknowledged and countered with fresh stories by which the postmodern self is able to re-narrate their own being. These fresh stories of atonement will acknowledge and deal meaningfully with the issue of chronic shame that exists in our postmodern times.

Shame, not guilt

Despite its extent and pervasiveness within the context of post-industrialized societies and the success of popular psychology and self-help manuals that seek to address it, shame is seldom heard about or discussed. Partly this is due to the fact that those who suffer from shame, while acutely aware of it and desperately searching for a way to vanquish themselves of it, find it almost impossible to speak its name. The fear of exposure, as we shall see, silences the victims of shame, so their true stories are seldom heard. Along with this fear, an equally frustrating problem in seeking to liberate the shamed person from their *dis-ease* is the fact that it is too easily absorbed into guilt-language. This is especially so within the Christian community, where shame is too often perceived merely as a rightful and necessary emotional response to the guilt we live under as disobedient children of God. However, this is perhaps a convenient collapsing of a more complex and highly misunderstood emotion into the simpler one of guilt, which fits more readily into our theological and ecclesiological practices. Sometimes, too, this chronic, personal, internalized condition is confused with the social and cultural emotion more commonly found in honour/shame societies such as Japan. The Christian community can be especially prone to confusing shame with this cultural phenomenon because the New Testament world is largely based on the social interplay and manoeuvring associated with honour/shame societies. However, to simply map this set of narratives onto our very different society, without considering the hermeneutical issues of historical and cultural context, can lead quite readily to misunderstanding, irrelevancy and even pastoral catastrophe.

Guilt and the type of shame generated within honour/shame societies, is a moral emotion. That is, it tends to be concerned with the 'Other', whether in the form of a neighbour, cultural expectation or social law. In this sense, guilt is a public emotion. As such, therapeutic liberation, or forgiveness of sins, requires some form of reparative action, which should, in theory, overcome feelings of guilt.

When we turn to the issue of chronic shame found within our post-industrialized societies, we observe an altogether different emotion. Shame in our context thrusts attention upon the self. While social setting and cultural expectations can cause shame, and even perpetuate it, in its post-industrialized form 'there is no need for an audience or the presence of others for people to feel shame'.[37] It is, in so many ways, an assessment of the self. The shamed person effectively ignores the 'Other' as the individual becomes acutely aware of his or her own internal struggles. The shamed person keeps interrelating and intimacy to a minimum to restrict the possibility of being exposed for who he or she truly is. This fear of exposure, coupled with a general sense of ontological badness or non-specific sense of wrong, conspires to paralyse the post-industrialized self in relation to the 'Other'. Therefore, the shamed person is either blinded to the possibility of (or the need for) reparative action or simply avoids it – most probably out of fear rather than ignorance or apathy.

'I' and the search for intimacy

Although the postmodern, post-industrialized self has a manifesto on relationship and craves intimacy, the subject of this relational pursuit is only ever 'I'. The agenda, often supported by their therapeutic advisors (professional and popular), is the pursuit of emotional and psychological health, self-satisfaction, security and justification of the actions they take to achieve these aims. The self does not seek intimacy because it is thinking about the need of the 'Other'; rather, the self is primarily looking to satisfy its own need. This is a subconscious action, but it is still a selfish one all the same. Therefore, this 'inability to take a serious interest in anything other than shoring up the self makes the pursuit of intimacy [with another] a futile endeavour'.[38] Again, Douglas Coupland, the archetypal postmodern author, gives an illustration from pop culture.

> I knew that unless I explored intimacy and shared intimacy with someone else then life would never progress beyond a certain point. I remember thinking that unless I knew what was going on inside someone else's head other than my own I was going to explode …

She says to me, but were we ever intimate? How intimate
were we really? … in the end did we ever really give each
other completely to the other? Do either of us even know
how to really share ourselves? … Imagine that I am drown-
ing and I reach within myself to save that one memory
which is me – what is it? Do you know? … What things
would each of us reach for? After all these years we just
wouldn't know.[39]

In this exchange, neither the husband nor the wife is
willing, or able, to give to the other in a mutual and
meaningful way. The self-centredness that permeates his
and her relating prevents the satisfaction from real
intimacy that each desires. Though the agenda of the individual is masked for a time and there is a temporary
belief that true intimacy has been found with another, the
reality is that the agenda is always 'local' – that is, all the
attention is upon the person's own drive to self-realization, even at the expense of the 'Other'. This tendency to
self-centredness may not be a conscious or deliberate act.
However, this does not alter the fact that once the 'Other'
discovers that the agenda in relating is always 'I' the
person becomes disillusioned, cynical about relationships and the real reasons for social interaction. Driven to
emotional, if not physical, isolation, this person begins to
manifest the same selfish tendencies, focusing solely
upon the self as the purpose for any social interaction
that may take place.

The postmodern self is driven by the twin desires of
therapeutic liberation and self-satisfying consumerism,
and one has to look no further than their day-to-day
interactions in post-industrialized societies to see these
desires clearly revealed. The centrifugal nature that
pushes away sin and guilt also pushes away the 'Other'.
The ironic impact of this drive to self-realization is,
however, that the resulting isolation leaves us with the

intensity of our own, self-critical gaze. Our need for love and intimacy that brings us a sense of worth turns against us and fuels the fires that led to chronic shame. Thus a vicious circle ensues: we long for intimacy, to have a deep sense of connectedness with ourselves and with 'Other(s)'. However, the project of self-realization ultimately pushes the 'Other' away. Alone, the project of self-realization collapses in on its/ourself, laying the seedbed for chronic shame to grow. Once mature, chronic shame stifles the post-industrialized self with doubts about the coherence of their very being and fears that he or she will be exposed for what they truly are – an incoherent being who neither trusts nor can be trusted to relate truthfully. With such fears the chronically shamed person hides behind masks, never truly connecting with others, never satisfying his or her need for intimate, mutual, undistorted relating – and so always falling short of what it means to be a human being, created in the image of the relational, Trinitarian God revealed in the Bible.

Shame and the absence of ontological coherence

Chronic shame is an intensely private affair. It heightens self-awareness and turns up the internal volume of self-consciousness. Those without such shame glide through day-to-day interrelating unaware of the self, unconcerned about the probable transparency with which they live before others. For the chronically shamed, however, this 'silent-self' 'is disrupted so that the self becomes "noisy" and the sole focus of attention. There is an acute sense of dividedness or doubleness as the self evaluates itself.'[40]

What the chronically shamed person craves above all else is a self-consistency; an ontological coherence; that is, a wholeness of being. This is all too often absent, however, due to a breakdown in their own personal story. For within the postmodern is a fissure dividing the story of the self. There is a disparity, an inconsistency, set up between the ideal-self (the person we aspire to be) of the postmodern and their real-self (the actuality of our lives). At the heart of shame, therefore, is the wronging of the self – specifically the ideal-self. The shamed person wants to live by the story of the ideal-self, or find a coherent story rather than an incoherent one. The purpose of mission is to allow people to see how the gospel can bring about this desire. Failure to live up to this ideal we hold for ourselves generates an emotional experience of self-deficiency.[41] So many of us are ontologically *incoherent* in the story we tell.

An emotionally charged scene from the Sam Mendes film *American Beauty* illustrates this self-deficiency and ontological incoherence, and its effect on the self.

> *Carolyn enters, alone. She's furious. She locks the sliding door and starts to pull the vertical blinds shut, then stops. Standing very still … she starts to cry: brief, staccato SOBS that seemingly escape against her will. Suddenly she SLAPS herself, hard.*
>
> CAROLYN: Shut up. Stop it. You … Weak!
>
> *But the tears continue. She SLAPS herself again.*
>
> CAROLYN: Weak. Baby. Shut up! Shut up! Shut up!
>
> *She SLAPS herself repeatedly until she stops crying. She stands, taking deep breaths until she has everything under control, then pulls the blinds shut, once again all business. She walks out*

calmly, leaving us alone in the dark, empty room. We HEAR CHEERING and APPLAUSE.[42]

This private outburst is triggered by Carolyn's perceived inability to live up to the demands of the ideal-self that she has constructed. From the perspective of her own personal narrative, she has exposed the story of her real-self – exposure being the great fear of the chronically shamed person. Here we find her distraught, trying to suppress the real-self, to subordinate it to the alternative, preferred story – her ideal-self.

Within this script, as is common among the chronically shamed, Carolyn finds no feelings of guilt for actions of social harm she has herself committed – actions that include adultery. Indeed, it could be suggested that she seeks self-justification for them. However, what becomes obvious is that she fears being exposed – not as an adulterer, but for who she *really* is – as a chronically shamed person, a self trying to live an unexposed life, fearful that others *will* 'notice' her and see the true self rather than the ideal. 'The self has a sense that it is defective and has a basic flaw that ensures its unacceptability and rejection by those whom it loves. Shame thus contains a fear of abandonment, loss of love, and so loss of self.'[43]

The shamed person does not feel like a person because he or she does not feel connected, not only with 'Others' but, more importantly, within themselves. The shamed virtually terrorize themselves, convinced that not only have they not 'lived up to their own standards and ideals but actually experience themselves as *embodying the anti-ideal*'.[44] They live with a debilitating incoherence of self, a breakdown between who they would like to be (their ideal-self) and the reality of who they are (their real-self). Therefore, to be 'healed' of chronic shame, the post-industrialized self must achieve self-connectedness, an ontological coherence.

Post-industrialized shame and social isolation

A continuum between modernity and postmodernity is that of the self as an autonomous and, to some extent, isolated individual. However, if we are to deal success-fully and meaningfully with the isolation of the postmodern self and so heal relational dysfunctions, we must not confuse the postmodern self with its modernist 'grandparents'. The drive to autonomy established by Enlightenment philosophy was, by and large, an isolation of free choice by the individual. What dis-tinguishes the post-industrialized, postmodern self from its modernist forebears is the fact that postmoderns are 'isolated because they cannot maintain interpersonal relationships, however desperately they try'.[45]

This inability to maintain interpersonal relationships is directly linked to the post-industrialized phenomenon of chronic shame. The reasons for this are complex, but they include the fear of exposure of the real-self and a lack of trust in the 'Other', which stems from a personal doubting of oneself. Isolated, the chronically shamed turn in on themselves. They can feel internally detached and unwanted by others. They begin to hide behind cover stories, false narrations of the self that they hope will allow some form of social interaction without the need to expose their real-self and be found wanting. However, such falsities stifle the potential of the self to reach a coherent selfhood and live with undistorted social intimacy.

Shame acts like a pollutant, poisoning every dimension of social interaction. Its toxin defiles the self so that the individual feels that he or she has become the very object of self and corporate derision. Such ontological self derision does not respond to puerile, popular Christian theology that too easily states: 'God loves the sinner but hates the sin.' Such sound bites may be easy to remember but they are theologically bankrupt, holding no meaning and therefore no atoning reality for the 'sinless' person living under the curse of chronic shame. For it is the person, their actual being, and not their actions, which is to blame for the social isolation they experience. This further distinguishes shame from guilt. Stephen Pattison helpfully observes that:

> Shame is self-related not object related. In guilt, the object of attention lies outside the self, in the person damaged or the act committed. In shame, on the other hand, the self is the object of concern. Indeed, one of the effects of shame is to exclude the outside world of other persons, events and actions and to fix attention firmly within the self.[46]

The chronically shamed fear exposing the reality that the way they narrate themselves to others is not their real-self. They are insecure in their relating, constantly aware of the need to cover the self from the 'Other' for fear of being found socially unacceptable. The shamed person lives in a permanent state of hiding, even when interacting with others. Only ever seeking to story their ideal-self, he or she never wants their real-self to be found. Despite the desire to seek significance and intimacy, the reality is that these fears become crippling and so the attention remains on the self in its search for significance rather than being open to the possibility that healing may actually be found in 'exposing' oneself to the 'Other', however painful or daunting that may seem.

As partially observed above, chronic shame stifles the post-industrialized self with doubts about the coherence of their very being and with fears that he or she will be exposed as one who neither trusts nor can be trusted to relate truthfully. This basic lack of trust in relating to self and to others generates and perpetuates shame. 'Chronically shamed people are inherently mistrustful of human relationships and of exposing themselves to others.'[47] The result is that shamed people are afraid to merge their lives, their personal stories, with others because of a fundamental lack of trust in relating.

In post-industrialized societies this is partly the result of our geographical and social fluidity. Few of us still live within the communities in which we were born and bred. Moving for reasons of higher education, career climbing, career hopping, the desire to live in the catchment area of a good school and less stable long-term relationships are all norms for the postmodern self. All that this creates, however, is a climate of anxiety, insecurity, doubt and uncertainty. 'Due to continuous change and mobility, all the individual has to hang on to is her own sense of self as she changes places, jobs and intimate relationships throughout life.'[48] Naturally, with such fluidity and lack of permanence, building the kind of trusting relationships the self needs is not easy. Indeed, the constant change of context is one of the primary reasons why the post-industrialized self constantly re-narrates the self to the point of confusion and incoherence. Aspirations need ideals – ideals not necessarily met by the real-self.

The post-industrialized self's failure to trust the 'Other' stems primarily and directly from the lack of trust we have in our own story. Shame is partly, or even largely, caused by our inability to live up to our ideal-self. Therefore, we don't trust our story because it isn't coherent and consistent. We presume others are the same.

Are we, then, really relating? As a result, we also lose the ability to trust others because we fear that they, too, suffer from the inability to trust and so are also unable to relate. To put it simply, if I know the story I am telling you is a 'cover' story, then the most sensible thing to do is presume that the self-story you are narrating does not tell me who you really are either. The chronically shamed live in the shadow of their cover story. This basic lack of trust leads us to a discourse on society that tells us quite simply that people are self-serving, just like ourselves, and so relate only to achieve self-satisfaction and self-justification.

Even unto death

Though a story is told, the chronically shamed person is in reality a 'silent' being. The real-self is seldom part of the story the postmodern tells, a self never spoken of. Only the ideal-self is ever heard in the social interactions of the chronically shamed post-industrialized self. The repression and hiding of the real-self, coupled with the fear of exposing it, lead inevitably to a life of silence before the 'Other'. Though the real-self exists, it lives the life of a mute, never daring to speak its name, barred from doing so by the crippling power of shame.

> Shame is a state of linguistic and social exclusion and alienation … one is trapped in the self without words and without other people: 'Shame sets one apart' and destroys the interpersonal bridge and social bonds between people. This may be felt as a kind of 'radical abandonment' as the person turns inward, loses social bonds and a sense of the other, and so, being a social animal, loses a real sense of self. The functioning social self is lost in shame. It is a lonely, alienating experience.[49]

The ultimate and longest silence, however, is surely death – unquestionably the fate of the postmodern self who suffers from an ontological incoherence brought about by chronic shame. Torn between the ideal- and the real-self, the postmodern's story collapses into utter meaninglessness – and utter meaninglessness is without doubt tantamount to death, for 'a self divided against itself cannot endure'.[50]

Metaphorically speaking, all who suffer the agony of chronic shame also suffer death – that is the entire and absolute collapse of the self. Shamed people are unable to relate without distortion. Putting it more strongly, they commit relational suicide, cutting their real selves off from every meaningful and potentially healing relationship. Pattison, again, records examples of people, 'changing address and not telling people where they have gone … as a way of escaping shame'.[51]

What the chronically shamed person is searching for is a way of 'deadening' the self, isolating, covering, suppressing, even banishing the self rather than have it exposed. While most manage to 'live' in this zombified state, some almost inevitably find the whole experience utterly unbearable. Shame must be put to death. But, as we have already observed, the self is the object of shame, not its subject. The 'sin' of shame cannot be isolated, confessed and dealt with so easily. The self and shame are indivisible; therefore the death of shame has to mean the death of self. For the chronically shamed self, the step from relational suicide to its physical counterpart can be very short indeed.

Though it ends here, with the sobering thought that shame (if it is not meaningfully and sufficiently dealt with) can ultimately lead to the 'death' of the chronically shamed person, this does not mean that we have exhausted this most complex of human *dis-eases* in this brief chapter. However, with such desperate finitude still in our minds, it is perhaps appropriate that our thoughts and discussions move closer to the real issue: how can we speak meaningfully and sufficiently to the chronically shamed post-industrialized self? How can the narratives surrounding the cross of Christ be understood as an atonement for a 'sinless' society?

3. Shame and Atonement: Some Issues to Consider

> I started by having a shower to cleanse my soul. Then I did some t'ai chi to rebuild my strength. Then I took some bach flower remedy of crab apple, which addresses shame and feeling inwardly dirty. Finally, I forgave myself for being human, weak and fallible.[52]

Atonement has on many occasions been described simply and helpfully as *at-one-ment*. Atonement removes division between two or more disparate entities so that they can be at one with each other. Despite the fact that the profoundly relational dimension of sin and atonement is not always as overtly present in our narratives as perhaps the biblical story would have it, the implied relational thrust contained in such a description lays a useful foundation on which to build if we are to address the issue of shame that parasitically eats away at the postmodern's ability to be *at one* not only with the 'Other' but, crucially, even with his or herself.

Unquestionably, Christian theology, especially that orientated around the atonement, has a well-developed notion of guilt and the rites and rituals deemed necessary to deal with it. Such tradition has served the church and its constituents well, especially in the guilt-ridden,

46

Christianized context that was pre- (and to a certain extent) post-Reformation Europe. However, with a high demand for absolution it is not surprising that the atonement became associated with functional processes rather than with the zenith of a dynamic relationship between Creator and created. Despite liturgies that reflected God's active immanence with his creatures, it was simply the knowledge of being pardoned from guilt that drove the purpose of the atonement for the pious.

In an increasingly 'sinless' society, where guilt is a marginal concern, even such functional views of the atonement are wholly inadequate in expressing the actuality of atonement. Indeed, so are many of the rites and rituals that address our sinfulness. What is needed is a fresh engagement with our story. We need to re-hear it in the light of the relational dysfunction – the debilitating, demoralizing and dehumanizing affects of chronic shame experienced by the post-industrialized self – and so understand its relevance to these issues. We must then seek to express, or re-tell, our story of atonement in such a way that it can be heard and meaningfully appropriated by the postmodern.

The fact is, recognized or not, the kind of chronic shame spelled out in the previous chapter is a central, dominant and pernicious theme in the story the post-industrialized self tells. Any individual or institution that claims to care for the well-being of the post-industrialized self, therefore, that ignores the existence of shame, is apathetic towards its victims or discounts its importance in the postmodern narrative, will ultimately be discredited. Failure to meaningfully address the ontological concerns of the post-industrialized self with our stories of atonement will only further marginalize the Christian community, for we will be a people without integrity. Indeed, as proved by the quote at the beginning of this chapter, without an active, atoning engagement with this vital concern, the chronically shamed post-modern will find others who are more than willing to bring their wisdom and stories of healing to their plight. There is, therefore, a clear and obvious challenge facing the church whose context is a shame-filled, post-industrialized, post-Christian society: 'We must ... acknowledge shame and thereby redeem it.'[53] However, this is not a straightforward concern. For while the problem is easy to establish, the solution is a much more difficult prospect.

> Shame is not easy to live with, to transcend, or to heal. There are no easy solutions or infallible techniques that can be applied. The condition of chronic shame is a hard one to ameliorate because individually and socially alienated people are, by definition, fundamentally cut off from the individuals and communities who might help them.[54]

Even without such isolation, this question still remains: How can a community help the chronically shamed person if the only narratives of healing and atonement they have to offer are ones based upon a reduction of sin and guilt to moral misdemeanour?

Finding resemblances

Shame is not sin. That is, it is not to be thought of as such if the only language we use to describe the phenomenon of sin is the breaking of a divine law, the wronging of others with subsequent feelings of personal guilt for doing so. This narrow description is wholly inadequate when seeking to speak meaningfully and sufficiently in a post-industrialized context. For while 'the biblical concept of sin includes the notion of disobedience ... this does not make acts of disobedience the foundation of our understanding of sin'.[55] Indeed, as we have already been persuaded, if described in this way, sin is not the currency of the postmodern narrative. To put it bluntly: the 'sinless' cannot exchange 'sin' for salvation. Their currency is shame – a harder problem to deal with, if only because our stories of atonement are insufficiently nuanced to allow the post-industrialized self to recognize their own plight within the stories that surround Jesus' life and death. This plight suffers the same relational consequences of sin, but only if sin is allowed to have its full semantic range. Then, and only then, will we begin to recognize that shame is a condition that Jesus would not only empathize with, but did indeed climb that much lamented hill to atone for.

What is needed is a fuller, more meaningful, more biblical account of the plight of humankind that speaks appropriately and often about the atonement as a restoration and reconciliation between relational beings, both human and divine, who too often live with an *absence* of mutual, intimate, undistorted relating. If we are to develop narratives of atonement from the stories that surround the life and death of Jesus, then it is imperative that we keep at the forefront of our theological creativity the reality that, for the chronically shamed postmodern self, relationships and ideals are more important and persuasive than law and punitive threat.

Of course, this is not an easy request to make, especially when we have surrounded the cross with powerful and convincing explanations of atonement that speak of the moral depravity of humankind and the sacrificial and substitutionary intervention of God to deal with such finite inadequacies. Indeed, in what is at times a very evil and depraved world, it is easy to understand why such a soteriology appeals. However, while we must not lose sight of any model of atonement that may bring reconciliation between Creator and creature, neither must we must inflate one over and against any other of the possible interpretations of Jesus' work – especially ones that can speak more meaningfully and salvifically as the gospel rubs up against ever-new contexts. This is precisely why we need to listen to the stories being told around us, to understand what it means to be a person living in a post-industrialized, post-modern, post-Christian world. But we also need to listen with a critical ear to the stories we tell as the Christian community, especially those that attempt to speak of the cross of Christ, and ask ourselves if these truly make sense within a post-industrialized context. This is not to ask 'Do they make sense to us?', but 'Do they have meaning for those who know not the atoning life and death of Jesus of Nazareth?'. Let us be clear, however, that 'making sense' is not a call to ditch biblical, theo-logical and doctrinal understandings of the atonement. It is the challenge to think creatively, laterally, tangentially, even abstractly, within the confines placed upon us, and to (re)tell our story with fresh and contemporary insight, while maintaining sufficient 'family resemblance' to claim a heritage within the boundaries of the Christian faith.

According to Stephen Pattison, 'Chronic shame, is best situated within the metaphorical ecology that pertains to defilement, pollution and stain.'[56] This, he argues, is in stark contrast with the metaphorical ecology surround-ing guilt, which has more to do with 'offence, debt and punishment'. Naturally, such things as offence or debt require equal and opposite responses, and so it is appro-priate to use language of punishment and reparation.

Shame, however, is far better described as a phenomenon that excludes, that pollutes the individual and community. It is therefore more appropriate to speak of cleansing and acceptance in order to be reconciled with the 'Other', as well as with one's own self. While guilty people need forgiveness, shamed people need a sense that they can live as whole, coherent beings – they need to live a story that makes sense so that they themselves make sense. But is this perhaps just another way of articulating what it means to be forgiven? What is certain is that exclusion and pollution more than adequately reflect the way sin is described in the Scriptures, while cleansing and acceptance are indeed the fruit of atonement.

Shame has no one, all-encompassing, quintessential reference that underlies all possible interpretations of the term as applied to the post-industrialized self. It is, and will remain, a complex, profound and pervasive human condition. Therefore, there has to be a certain amount of generalization and synthesis in the account we give of shame, for like most human emotions it is multifarious rather than formulaic in nature. That said, there are common threads among these differing views about shame that allow us to see with a certain amount of clarity the problem before us, enabling the church to address chronic shame with an explanation of atonement and to bring healing to some, if not to all.

This is helpful because it allows us to reflect on the fact that we could just as easily speak of sin in the same way – as a complex, profound and pervasive human condition. Regardless of whether sin is original or not, any harmatology that seeks to define or describe sin simplistically or in its entirety is unhelpful. That is because sin, like shame, is a relational issue and is therefore irreducible to formulaic descriptions. However, there are family resemblances, similar consequences and therefore a common solution to the issues sin and shame raise. The person suffering from chronic shame is all too aware of the human condition – not as a 'sinner', guilty of disobedience to a divine law, but as a being who lives with a dysfunction in their relating. Therefore, it is appropriate that we look to the atoning work of Jesus, and the narratives that surround his life and death, in order to seek some form of resolution to the problem of shame.

The problem of being pre-social and pre-moral

Shame generates the 'sinless' society – not in reality, but in perception. But it is the perception that is most real to the psyche of the postmodern mind. It is this story that has to be met with our narratives of atonement because it is this story that shapes the postmodern. The chronically shamed, 'sinless' self needs to be saved – not from divine wrath, but from self-judgement, which isolates and alienates the self from (each) 'Other'. They are emotionally, socially and spiritually paralysed by an inability to trust, to commit and to believe in themselves or others. Therefore, the postmodern self lives at the boundaries of intimate, fulfilling, healing, social inter-action. They entertain and flirt with ideas of community and all that such human interaction demands, but in reality they are isolated, socially immature, even emasculated.

Such social isolation raises a contentious, yet extremely poignant and pragmatic issue regarding the chronically shamed self and our narratives of atonement. For sin, as we have indicated already, is largely understood and communicated (especially in popular Christian parlance) as a wronging of a holy God, disobedience to a divine law – a law that ultimately defines the community of God. By these things we know we are sinners and are able, so we believe, to communicate such sinfulness to others and therefore their need of atonement. Rather controversially, however, the dilemma we face in speaking about the plight of people in this way is that the chronically shamed, 'sinless' self does not psychologically or narratively fit into this worldview. The self-stories they tell, which isolate them from meaningful, human interface, effectively turn them into *a-moral* or, perhaps more accurately, *pre-moral*, beings. For it is not that they could care less about issues of morality, it is a far more desperate plight: due to their inability to live lives of mutual, intimate, undistorted relating they become trapped within themselves, cut off from the moral community. They are quite literally *pre-social* as well as *pre-moral*. 'They are not other-regarding and moral in the sense of being able to take properly defined and limited responsibility for their own actions and then being able to execute them.'[57]

Naturally this has rather radical implications if we are to form appropriate and meaningful narratives of atonement for the chronically shamed, 'sinless' self. For to speak of guilt, to make moral judgements about the post-industrialized self in relation to a divine or indeed a communal law, is to tell a story that makes no sense to this self. We need meaningful stories to communicate the saving actions of Christ because an irrelevant and inadequate story of atonement is not only pointless, it is tragic.

Given this immediate observation about the social and psychological condition of the chronically shamed person, a meaningful and appropriate story of atonement must be one that speaks dynamically and specifically to the plight of the post-industrialized, 'sinless' self as the self perceives it, and not as we would wish to describe it. It is therefore necessary to orientate our narratives of atonement so that they address the issues of shame, and not of 'sin' and guilt. We also need (taking our cue from Karl Barth) to accept that only those who have already been atoned for and reconciled to the 'Other' know what it is to have sinned, to feel guilt at the wrong they have done – however challenging an idea this may be.[58] For until the chronically shamed, postmodern self has been able to deal with their relational *dis-ease* and has sufficiently re/joined society and/or the community of faith, that person will never be in a position to understand and take real responsibility for the relational dysfunction that categorizes his or her life as shame-filled. Strange as it may sound, we need to think of atonement as something that brings about a 'shameless' society. Therefore, as a community of faith that has been gifted with the responsibility of retelling the story through witness, liturgy and action, we should be working towards being a 'shameless' community – and that requires reconciliation and atonement prior to dealing with issues of moral sin and guilt. Only then can the chronically shamed make sense of the demand to '*Go, and sin no more.*' Until that time, they will remain *pre-social, pre-moral*, chronically shamed people.

Confession and the fear of exposure

We are already aware that shame, or perhaps more precisely the fear of being exposed as an incoherent being, has the very powerful affect of silencing the post-industrialized self so that he or she is unable to tell who they really are, preferring instead to story an ideal-self to all they encounter. This fear can be so powerful that some will go 'missing' or even commit suicide, rather than live such an alienating and meaningless life. Though the argument here is that the atonement brought about by the life and death of Jesus is a meaningful and sufficient reality that deals with chronic shame, this unwillingness by the victim to expose the real-self, to embrace the reality of shame and tell their story openly, generates a significant impasse. The problem is that the processes by which the individual is usually called to appropriate the atonement for his or herself requires some form of confession, usually verbal in nature, before forgiveness and reconciliation can take place.

Of course, public storytelling, or confession, is not a common event even for those who may be more comfortable, willing and able to expose themselves in this way. Quite simply we live in a context where the structures of society leave little space for human beings to tell their stories. Storytelling is stunted by a lack of public arena and the desire for consumerism and entertainment based around television and surfing the net. However, even if we did live in communities that were more comfortable with the idea of individual and public orality, the problem of chronic shame would remain a big hurdle for the individual contemplating storytelling or confession.

Much of Western Christianity (Protestant Christianity in particular), through liturgies and its confessional nature, has emphasized the fundamental sinfulness of human beings in relation to God. This story of depravity and guilt has been told, over and over again. (Whether it has been told helpfully or to great effect is a debatable issue that is beyond the scope of this particular argument, except to say that an unhealthy focus upon the self, even as a sinner before God, serves to emphasize self-consciousness, self-awareness and even self-centredness – the very causes and outcomes of chronic shame.) However, this retelling has kept a particular story of what it means to be human in the popular psyche, which has allowed the traditions and interpretations of the atonement to be generally understood, if not always successfully appropriated, by the masses.

The problem this has left us with in a 'sinless' society is that too often these Christian traditions propagate rather than assuage the destructive nature of chronic shame. With regards to the liturgies, theologies, symbols and stories with which we surround the atonement, whatever our understanding or intentions, it is how the hearer perceives them and relates to them that is the issue – and not how we interpret them. Because of this, 'there is no aspect of Christian thought or practice that might not engender or exacerbate shame in some individual or group'.[59] With sin or guilt there is at least the potential for a cathartic experience to take place, for us to relate our wrongdoing, receive forgiveness and be reconciled to the society we have wronged or to the god whose anger we have raised. However, 'the primary victim of shame is the self, and there is nothing that one can do by some intentional act (e.g. of confession or atonement) to alleviate the pain'.[60] The postmodern self is ensnared by shame. Shame is a story we find difficult to relate and discuss with others because, as we do so, we relive the experience and compound shame still further. Therefore exposure, through confession, will only cause a deepening of the shame experience. The polarity between the ideal- and the real-self will be widened. The ontological coherence craved by the postmodern is actually hindered by confession (in the general sense of revealing a reality about ourselves). The possibility of the self being brought into a meaningful, reconciling and healing relationship with his or herself and the 'Other' is beyond question. For the chronically shamed, the fear of exposure caused by confession places the possibility of atonement in jeopardy.

As we have seen, chronic shame is experienced as if it is a pollutant. It defiles the self, bringing a self-imposed isolation and exclusion. Healing from shame therefore requires opportunity for cleansing, for inclusion and social reincorporation and relational restoration. These are concepts that fit comfortably with biblical ideas of atonement and so should be important themes within our stories of the cross. However, 'the cleansing rituals that were available to the ancients'[61] are few and far between in the post-industrialized West. With such an impasse facing us it may well be fruitful to consider how we may incorporate cleansing rites and ritual, rather than verbal acts of confession and repentance, back into our corporate expression of the story of Jesus. We may even have to consider making room for the 'sinless' to respond as they wish – so that, at least initially, they can do so without fear of being exposed.

The process of atonement

Finally, if only briefly, I wish to consider the idea of the process of atonement. For though we might speak of the cross as a once and for all sacrifice of atonement, *the* most significant moment in salvation history, a point in time that fundamentally changed the way humanity would and could relate to the divine, this does not mean that all people will be able to hear the gospel once, respond to it with repentance and feel that their lives have been significantly altered by this brief encounter. For some, it is a long, painful journey to accept the story of atonement so that it significantly changes their lives.

For the chronically shamed, it is perhaps better to imagine the atonement as a process rather than a crisis event. 'There are no sure, certain, or quick ways of healing shame ... "At best it is a creative and compassionate art."'[62] For while the more rational and objective nature of guilt can be dealt with in a moment of confession and absolution, the more personal and relational dynamics of chronic shame, resulting in mistrust, fear, alienation and isolation, mean that the task of atonement in reconciling the person to self and to the 'Other' is more akin to a long and arduous journey.

Atoning for shame is a process that leads us towards wholeness. For while there is a once and for all act that opens the possibility of reconciliation, healing and fullness, *at-one-ment* for the chronically shamed is achieved only via a series of 'moments' that move them to a place where they can live without the distorted relating that has become so much part of the story they tell. Such moments need, therefore, to be made available to the chronically shamed person through the creation of safe, non-intrusive, non-judgmental spaces and communities that allow the chronically shamed, 'sinless' self to hear meaningful and sufficient stories of atonement and so, via storytelling, symbolic action and ritual, come to find the ontological coherence, the *at-one-ment*, that so tragically alludes them.

There is, however, no easy solution to such difficulties. But then simplicity is not a luxury we are afforded when dealing with the complexities of people as relational beings. Indeed, is it not the biblical witness that the reconciliation of God to humankind, and humankind to ourselves, is a long and arduous process?

From all we have said here, it appears obvious that if we are to deal meaningfully and sufficiently with the issue of chronic shame as one of the most dominant themes in the story 'What it means to be human', what is needed is a critical reassessment of our stories of atonement. Naturally, it would be unreasonable and untenable to suggest that our traditions and liturgies as they currently stand be 'ceremonially' dumped in favour of new ones – though perhaps there is a strong case to be made for at least working towards more helpful and meaningful liturgies [something we shall return to later in Part IV]. Indeed, 'There will never be a time when the themes [of sin and guilt and the models of atonement needed to deal with such human tragedies will be] wholly irrelevant, because the anxieties they address are perennial.'[63]

That Jesus' death deals with sin as our disobedience and guilt is self-evident. That Jesus' death also deals with shame goes unnoticed through ignorance and myopia in our understanding and communication of the work of Jesus in the atonement. Therefore, if the church it is to speak meaningfully and sufficiently as the community which gathers around the cross of Christ, it needs to draw out fresh emphases from its traditions, from its theologies and liturgies, to show new facets of its narratives that allow the chronically shamed and the 'sinless' self to recognize their plight and hear a story of hope and healing – a story of atonement (*at-one-ment*) that they can appropriate for their own plight.

II

The Function of Narrative

Story, Self and the Shape of
Things to Come

4. Narrative Now

Narratives ... give a coherence to human lives.[64]

So far we have sketched in some detail the loss of sin in our post-industrialized context and the subsequent rise of the 'sinless' society with its deep-seated issue of chronic shame and its social and relational consequences. In doing this, however, much has been made of the importance of narrative and story in the shaping of the self. Indeed, there has been an assumption that the reader would, for the present moment at least, buy-in to the rather bold claims being made about story to allow the discussion to focus more readily on sin and shame. However, given that much more will be made of the importance of story in shaping the self (especially as we move towards a rereading of the narratives that surround the life and death of Jesus), we will take an 'excursion' at this stage to consider at some length the centrality of narrative in a postmodern context.

Though our discussion has taken us into the realm of chronic shame as the plight of the post-industrialized self, this is merely a specific example of a more general sense of meaningless, emptiness and alienation felt by the postmodern. With only one life to live, and that getting longer with each generation, peoples of the post-industrialized developed world are far more concerned with this life than with their fate in the next – and that is where story comes in. Narrative, or the desire to tell stories about the world and ourselves, is the mode by which people try to make sense of the one life they have. People look to stories for a quality of sufficiency, an explanation of the joys and the ills that life brings. That is why, as we have said, if we desire the postmodern to 'hear' our stories of atonement, and appropriate them as narratives of salvation, then they must be stories that are meaningful and sufficient. However, while narratives do give coherence to the self (or, to put it more forcefully: to be a person is to have narrative coherence), to speak in this way only adds weight to the argument being posited here. That is, while narrative (or ontological) coherence may be desired, many people live, or merely 'exist', with a narrative 'in-coherence' – a breakdown in the story they are able to tell, which results in a disruption of self.

Given this contemporary dilemma, we shall go on to discuss the role narrative plays in an increasingly therapeutic society before considering how the Christian community might similarly and judiciously appropriate narrative when speaking meaningfully and sufficiently about the atonement. For the moment, however, our attention will remain with a more general look at narrative and its increasing significance in shaping what has become a post-industrialized, post-Christian, post-modern society.

The pervasiveness of narratives

It is now almost universally accepted by the academic community that human beings are storytellers.

Anthropology, sociology and, more recently, psycho-therapy, are drawn to the fact that, without exception, all peoples, past and present, have made sense of the world through story. That said, story remains for many an uncertain and dubious way of expressing knowledge. It is part of an epistemology that is given over to fiction, myth and primitive ways of understanding and de-scribing the world. Its role in speaking about certainties, in stating truth and fact is, to say the least, unclear.

Post Enlightenment, the ability of the self to reason – to name the world and its contents in an assured manner – suppressed the claims of myth and story as a way of knowing, relegating them to mere fictions in a world of certainties. Naturally, this had huge implications for religious traditions that had communicated for so long through myth and parable, narrative and allegory. By the time we reached the twentieth century, modernity's grip upon Western society was as strong as the West's imperial-, colonial-, and industrial-grip on the rest of the developing world. The industrialized-post-Enlighten-ment-self stood at the apex of evolution, placed there by a scientific worldview that spoke the language of reason, rationality and logic.

Unsurprisingly, fearful of the hubristic claims of modern, scientific man and the debunking of religious epistemologies, the church responded in kind, de-veloping logical apologetics and modernistic, scientific, hermeneutical methodologies. The truth and fact of the Christian faith (if this is not oxymoronic) became the basis of mission and evangelism in this emerg-ing context. The biblical 'story' was largely sidelined. Of greater concern was historical authenticity, for such facts were thought to be far more persuasive for the modern, rational mind than talk of myth and metaphor.

This is not by way of criticism, however. Though some may find it hard to accept, the church has always been as influenced by the cultural and philosophical context in which it has found itself as it has by any commitment to the Scriptures. Indeed, it could be suggested that to be *in* the world, culturally and philosophically, could be positively beneficial to its missional work, rather than detrimental. However, problems certainly arise during stark periods of transition if we allow cultural and philosophical expression to accelerate away from us. For this is when the relevance and meaningfulness of our message stretch to breaking point. This is when the language we use to communicate becomes unintelligible and incredulous to our cultural and philosophical contemporaries. This is a very real danger currently facing the church as we journey deeper into the twenty-first century.

The dominant grip that modernity had on our cultural and philosophical thinking has finally begun to weaken. The West has become post-imperial, post-colonial, post-industrial – postmodern. And the self, who slips through the ever-widening fingers of modernity, falls into a world of uncertainty where truth and untruth, fact and fiction, history and myth are one and the same thing. In this world you are only human if you have a story to tell and a storied world in which to live. Indeed, narrative is no longer something which is imposed upon the world and the self, but the self and the world are narrative in their very existence. 'We dream in narrative, daydream in narrative, remember, anticipate, hope, despair, believe, doubt, plan, revise, criticize, construct, gossip, learn, hate and love by narrative.'[65]

Far from being a peripheral in our perception of self and the world, story is now seen very much as a pervasive, necessary and constructive epistemological category. The academy (and that includes the scientific community) is waking up to this reality and it is, to an increasing degree, using narrative in its work. The assured world of reason is slowly but surely being transferred to the realm of myth, which, in turn, has been raised from a place of derision by epistemologists to a necessary tool in understanding what it is to be human. The issue is no longer whether something is mere fact, but whether we can any longer speak of something as being mere story. For even the most 'simple' story is entrenched in a complex network of interrelated parts. With our eyes wide open to the role story plays in making us human, '[even] the most familiar, most primitive, most ancient and seemingly straightforward of stories reveal depths that we might hitherto have failed to anticipate'.[66]

Such fresh insight has made it clear that to speak of story in purely fictional terms does an injustice to it as a medium for speaking about, understanding and shaping the world in which we live. We have sufficiently recognized the complexities and centrality of story and myth such that we can no longer allow them to be side-lined, 'even for a culture as fragmented, sophisticated, and anti-traditional as ours'.[67] For the time being, story's place in the human activity of telling is as assured as reason was at the beginning of the twentieth century.

Narrative and the postmodern self

When a human being narrates the self, that individual is not imposing his or her will upon reality and shaping it in a fictitious manner. Rather, they are simply augmenting a world that is itself narrative. The narrative self has been pre-empted. 'Life is always-already narrative, in advance of our narration.'[68] Empirical knowledge, the idea of *quod erat demonstrandum* given to us by the Enlightenment, finds itself merely a supplement to the more experiential realities of the postmodern. We are no longer convinced simply by our ability to demonstrate that something is so; the more important epistemology is for reality to be *lived as if it were so*.

What the postmodern self has come to believe is that formulaic, rational cognition makes for poor language when describing the complexities of human action and interaction. Narrative is far better suited to a way of knowing and interpreting the day-to-day experiences of life that we need to make meaningful. It is like a thread that holds together what can be at times the rather disparate parts of our lives, weaving them into the story of who we are. Therefore, story should never be seen as an irrelevant or neutral phenomenon, as some primitive way of knowing that has been outmoded by rational epistemologies. Indeed, story is for the postmodern self a most powerful present and future-shaping reality.

Despite the fact that story appears to be based around questionable, experiential ways of understanding our-selves and the world around us, such as intuition and emotion, the postmodern prefers to trust these inner ways of knowing over and above the public 'truths' given by archaic institutions. Though many of our post-Enlightenment ancestors preferred to follow Kant in downplaying emotions, including the development of a more rational faith, we cannot escape the fact that we are, first and foremost, sensual beings. For the postmodern, intuitive and emotional ways of knowing are far more important than logic in giving account of truth. Briefly put, *the postmodern self prefers a good story to a good fact*. Even the eminent scientist E.O. Wilson has recognized that 'No matter ... how beautifully *theory* falls out to however many decimal places, all our experience is still processed by the sensory and nervous systems … and all of knowledge is still evaluated by our idiosyncratically evolved emotions.'[69]

Of course, context plays a large part in the formation of emotional and intuitive ways of knowing. It would be very naïve indeed to ignore this stark fact. Context contributes to interpretation and meaning. Our personal story is influenced by the collective narratives of the communities in which we live. Indeed, the factors of gender, class, race and sexual preference are powerful contributors to the story we tell. Nevertheless, none of this detracts from the reality that, regardless of how it is formed, or what influences shape it, we must engage with the personal story told by the post-industrialized self if we are to understand the postmodern.

What is not being suggested here is that rational, logical epistemologies are a complete irrelevance in our post-industrialized context. Indeed, despite academic agreement about the pervasiveness of narrative among human beings, no one is keen to make narrative unique, or the prime way of knowing and expressing knowledge. Even narrative thinkers, while favouring story as a significant approach to reality, recognize that human expression and interpretation are not limited to storytelling. We are more than capable of organizing and recollecting life in non-narrative form. However, the fact that narrative is so pervasive must surely silence criticism, which suggests that the current attention given to story, and its significance for speaking about reality, is disproportionate to other epistemologies Its common-ness alone demands that it be taken seriously.

However, notwithstanding its new-found attention, the very pervasiveness that gives significance to story is also one of its weaknesses, for the complexity and diversity of narrative forms have meant that, 'despite their agreement on the importance of the category, there is yet to emerge a consensus among narrative thinkers concerning precisely what the term narrative means'.[70] Such an issue could easily lead to digression in this discussion. So to simplify matters, and to use narrative in a clear and productive way, we will refer to it with the presupposition that narrative is 'an account of characters and events in a plot moving over time and space *through conflict towards resolution'*.[71] These most basic elements of emplotment are often referred to as the grammar of a story, without which it ceases to be a story. As S.W. Sykes states when referring to the narrative at the heart of the Eucharist, 'Story is only a story if it possesses a setting, a theme, a plot, and a resolution; it is memorable only if it conforms to this natural sequence.'[72]

Story also draws on the grammar of symbol and metaphor. These decorate the plot, drawing readers/ hearers deeper into the storied world and helping them to make sense of it. Metaphor and symbol are appealing to the human senses – they attract. As Becker notes, a human being, 'is not just a blind glob of idling protoplasm, but a creature with a name who lives in a world of symbols and dreams and not merely matter.'[73] Through the grammar of symbol and metaphor, story is able to speak the language of, and be understood by, the human psyche. This has particular significance for the postmodern, who typically constructs the idea of self and the world through sign, symbol and metaphor.

Metanarrative and the postmodern self

We have already made, like many postmodern theorists, rather far-reaching claims about the role of narrative in the construction of the post-industrialized self. Along with Payne, it appears reasonable to argue that, 'in a postmodern perspective ... stories or narratives form the matrix of concepts and beliefs by which we understand our lives, and the world in which our lives take place.'[74] The question often raised, however, is whether the metanarrative (and that includes those of religious purpose) can ever be meaningfully and sufficiently brought to bear upon the typically isolated, localized, personalized and pluralistic narratives of the post-modern self? After all, it should be self-evident that our lives are multi-storied rather than the product of a single, all-encompassing drama. Indeed, given that there are so many stories and that we can interpret similar events in different ways, the claim that no single story can be free of ambiguity or contradiction, nor encapsulate or handle all contingencies of life, appears to be a reasonable assumption. Given these observations, it is easy to understand the postmodern's derision of the metanarrative.

Perhaps the first thing to point out is that while the postmodern self may not live comfortably with the idea of the metanarrative, he or she is not ignorant of its existence nor, to greater or lesser degrees, able to remove him or herself from its influence. As was suggested earlier, even though they may baulk at the idea, the post-modern is rooted to a form of metanarrative – that of Romanticism. The postmodern is quite simply a storyteller, 'living among the ruins of ... former grand narratives ... [making] stories out of the rubble of the old narratives [they] find lying around'.[75] While they may perceive only the 'little' stories of their own world, this cannot detract from the reality that they are in a world where all the little stories are simply part of a larger narrative. Like all movements, postmodernism is nothing more than the search for self-understanding and, if postmoderns are to understand themselves, then they cannot escape the metanarrative entirely. Indeed, despite it infamous incredulity towards the metanarrative, postmodernism is itself nothing more than 'a grand narrative, announcing the death of another grand narrative in its rearview mirror'.[76]

Even if this derision for the metanarrative remains, it does not mean that the Christian story has to keep silent. It can, and has, been argued that Christianity is as much a complex drama of little stories as it is a metanarrative that should be embraced in its entirety. Brueggemann has noted, for instance, that 'as the Bible does not consist in a single large drama, but in many small, disordered dramas, so our lives are not lived in a small single, large, unified drama'.[77] The postmodern life is a story consisting of a number of chapters that are related only by the fact that they are lived out by one person. Therefore, in order to prove meaningful and sufficient, the task of the Christian narrative would not be 'a grand scheme or a coherent system, but the voicing of a lot of little pieces out of which people can put life together in fresh configurations'.[78]

Brueggemann certainly gives food for thought with his observations. However, there is an underlying dilemma that he does not address. For while he recognizes the chameleon-like ability of the postmodern, post-industrialized self to 'sensitively [adjust] the "presentation of self" in relation to whatever is demanded of a particular situation',[79] his observation does not deal with the desire for ontological consistency. It does not give coherence to the self-story but only perpetuates its fragmented, traumatic and ultimately meaningless state. And if left unattended, as we have been at pains to point out, such incoherence ultimately leads the postmodern into the depths of chronic shame.

That said, without blurring the issue to utter abstraction this is not to argue that one needs a 'single' coherent story – only that the self is able to deal coherently with the multivocity with which he or she may choose (or be forced) to narrate the self. An inability to deal with this multivocity, however, is precisely the inadequacy we observe in the chronically shamed between the ideal- and real-self.

This is my story, now tell me yours

Once upon a time … humankind understood everything through stories. Unlike the 'How?' that drove the philosophical and scientific pursuits of the Enlightenment, stories were employed to help satisfy the 'Why?' of human curiosity. 'The answers they gave did not have to be literally true; they only had to satisfy people's curiosity by providing an answer, less for the mind than for the soul. For the soul they were true, but probably no one bothered to ask whether that truth was factual or "merely" metaphorical.'[80] With the emergence of post-modernity and the concerns of the post-industrialized self, we have come full circle. No longer convinced by the rational icons of modernity – $e=mc^2$ – the post-industrialized self is instead looking to story 'avidly for illumination of [their] homelessness in time and circumstance'.[81]

Though many are comfortable living this way, there will be for some (perhaps many in the church) a question that rings in the void that is perceived to exist between the objective certainties of truth and the more subjective, relativistic understanding that story is believed to give. Unfortunately, there is no reassurance that can be given to those who desire to make statements of fact derived from a particular metanarrative. There is 'truth' for the post-industrialized self: 'this is my truth; now tell me yours'. Relativism reigns. The postmodern self approaches metanarratives of past and present institutions, as well as claims to be singular holders of truth, with extreme caution. There is a vacuum of meaning at the heart of our post-industrialized societies. However, what postmodernity has done is to liberate stories 'from the tyranny of having to be legitimized by a metanarrative before they can be taken seriously'.[82] In postmodernity all stories have equal and potential worth as narratives which may bring meaning and illumination to the life being lived. Therefore, a story told by a person in his or her own words of his or her own experience does not have to plead its case before all other narratives, since this is 'truth' for that person, at that given moment in his or her life. A story is, therefore, legitimized by its usefulness – or, to speak negatively, a story is delegitimized if it proves meaningless. The only way to legitimately question this storied reality, relative as it may seem, is to offer an alternative story: 'This is my story, now tell me yours.'

The postmodern, post-industrialized self lives in a sea of stories. Being consumers as they are, postmoderns will 'try on for size' any story they encounter that might prove meaningful and sufficient. In this sense, they are open to stories that may have been previously associated with the truth claims of the metanarratives of religious traditions – but only if they encounter them as narratives and not as statements of fact. It is of paramount importance, therefore, that as a church we let our story be a story and not a mere fact. For the postmodern, facts are soulless, lacking the relational dynamic that gives personal, appropriate and sufficient meaning to the

'Why?' of life. Therefore, if we believe that our story is the most meaningful and sufficient one that can be encountered, it will be revealed as the 'truth' without us having to state it as such.

5. Narrative Possibilities

Every 'telling' of myself is a retelling, and the act of telling changes what can be told next time.[83]

History tells us that the world we live in is not a static place but one that changes. There are, of course, many reasons for this fluidity. However, in terms of significance for our concerns here, there is perhaps no reason more important than our own ability to imagine the world to be different from the way it is, thereby opening up the possibility of changing it. Indeed, it has even been suggested that 'what appears to distinguish us humans from all other species is the ability to conceive of things being different from the way they are'.[84] This ability is linked directly to that other uniquely human characteristic, storytelling. That is because narrative has an innate capacity to construct, deconstruct and reconstruct the world. To tell a story is not simply to describe what is already there but also to conjure with the possible, to hint at, to suggest, even create futures that can be entered. For human beings at least, the world can be changed by alternative narration – and so can the identity of the self that dwells in this world of narrative possibility, for it too exists in the present and is shaped in the future via storytelling.

To live as a storied-self, in a sea of actual and potential stories, is to stir the imagination, which is the human capacity to depict, render, accept and rehearse the world in an alternative way, to consider other possibilities to those currently on offer. To be a storied-self is to live life as an 'open' being. Until we succumb to the finality of death, our lives are functioning yet incomplete stories of who we are. Therefore, consciously or subconsciously, we are open to the possibility of change, even on a daily basis, as we encounter alternative and potential ways of narrating the self. We consider entering into a world which is not currently our own, or becoming someone other than who we are at this present moment in time. Narratives project possible worlds, alternatives we can consider. They allude to potential ways of living that may bring the 'good life' we crave. Therefore, built into the narratives that invade our lives is an element of hope, that most wonderful of human incentives, which challenges us to assess our own story, perhaps tired or imprisoning, in the light of the new.

Such characteristics will form the foundation on which we will build what we hope will be an insightful and fruitful engagement between the Gospels as narratives of atonement and the story of the post-industrialized self, living in a 'sinless' society yet searching for narrative coherence to heal chronic shame. For the moment, however, we turn our attention to the relatively new, yet increasingly common, field of narrative therapy. This is not because the plight of the post-industrialized self is a matter purely of psychological concern – though we must not be quick to dismiss this dimension. A consideration of narrative therapy will, rather, deepen our understanding of story and how it can be appropriated in meaningful and sufficient ways.

Narrative therapy

For the post-industrialized self, the therapist is like a new messiah, come to vanquish oppression and torment. Whether achieved through direct access to a professional psychotherapist or mediated through magazine-format TV and self-help volumes, the liberation of the self through psychological insight is the desire of the faithful. However, the processes by which healing and wholeness are understood to come about are as varied and colourful as the magazines and TV shows through which the therapist reaches 'clients'. Even the more professional and serious psychotherapists, who have their clients referred to them by GPs, social services, and so on, follow various theories and methods in order to bring about the same end – a meaningful and sufficient resolution to the mental, behavioural or emotional plight their client faces.

Many therapists understand their work to be based upon rational, logical, observable methodology. As healers of people, some even consider that they belong to a branch of medicine and are therefore working out of a scientific epistemology, or worldview. Nevertheless, as we have already begun to suggest, the metanarrative that science is the key to all our futures is going through a crisis. Despite the historic influence of scientific methodology upon psychotherapy, there is a growing hesitancy among practitioners to see this as the source of all reality. Notwithstanding a methodology based upon a claimed scientific heritage, much psychotherapy is moving away from the 'laboratory' and into the realms of storied realities.

Like all movements for change, the therapeutic transfer to narrative is driven partly from within the profession and is partly a response to changing attitudes from without. By its own definition therapy needs to be narrated because it is 'a means by which individual members of that culture engage with the question of what it means to be a person at the specific time and place in history in which they find themselves',[85] and in this time and place in history the person is a storied-self. Indeed, in many ways the process of therapy has always been narrative based. Even those therapists who would not wish to think of themselves as engaging narratively with their clients are, at the very least, following what can easily be described as a basic story plot. That is, they are engaged in the active process of moving an account of a character (their client), and the events of this character's life, over time and space through conflict towards resolution.

The flip side of this internal awakening within the therapeutic community is a fundamental change in attitude among the typical constituents of the therapist: the peoples who live in post-industrialized societies. As briefly discussed, for myriad reasons the post-industrialized self, while reaping the benefit of scientific and technological advance, doubts the supposed 'good' intentions of those who narrate the world through science. Therefore, in order to keep a 'clientele', it has proven necessary for the therapeutic community to 'retell' their own story in order to connect, or more accurately reconnect, meaningfully and sufficiently with the plight of the post-industrialized self by speaking a common language – the language of the narrative. This awakening to the 'new age' in which people narrate their identity has come along with the emergence and embracing of a therapeutic technique that recognizes this – narrative therapy.

Though the idea of using narrative in therapeutic endeavour is a relatively new one, the psychoanalysts themselves make no claim to uniqueness. Indeed, they understand their job as simply recognizing cultural change, being aware of the implications that such changes bring to the construction of the self and acknowledging the means by which individuals, at any given time, are seeking to make sense of themselves and the world around them. This attitude has led them to recognize the current desire to narrate the self and the world and to grasp and employ techniques that acknowledge the reality that narrative can be used to conflict with and *convert* the worldviews and dominant stories of any given individual who is struggling to make sense of their dysfunction. The therapist's success in the adaptation and adoption of such cultural changes should therefore be seen not as a threat, but as a constructive challenge to other communities, such as the Christian church, who also wish to engage meaningfully and sufficiently within the current post-industrialized context.

Employing the counter-narrative

As it is frequently remarked, identity is an act of narration for the postmodern self. George Stroup's is typical of this sort of observation: 'it is no accident that when they are asked to identify themselves most people recite a narrative or story'.[86] Identifying the self as a storied entity has become an important starting point for narrative therapy. Indeed, so powerful is the idea of narrative as the reality-shaping, preferred mode of expression for humankind that it is not unreasonable to suggest that without a storied-self, a person cannot claim to be a person. That said, this is a hypothetical concern. To be human *is* to account for our existence, quite literally, by narration. The real issue, therefore, is not finding a story to tell but rather the content of the stories we actually do tell – what storied plight shapes who we are. The concern of narrative therapy is that too many of the stories we use to shape who we are have become narratives of torment or, as in the case of chronic shame, cover stories – narratively projected ideals to throw others off the scent to protect us from the fear that they may find our real self and despise us.

If there is a failure to perform adequately, shame is an ever-present danger lurking in the wings and cutting to the centre of personal esteem and identity. In this context, it is not surprising that personal therapy may take a crucial role as overexposed selves try to become the depredations of shame. However, therapy has a more fundamental role as the 'routine art of self-observation' that allows the construction of the narrative of the self and enhances self-control.[87]

This is a useful observation. For not only does it shed light on the importance of narrative in the healing of chronic shame, but it also makes the point that narrative therapy is not the application of an alien process to the human psyche, rather that it is simply enhancing therapeutically a process that is already present and active in our lives: the retelling, or re-storying of the self. Indeed, the process of creating a self by plotting a story that is always being retold is an ordinary and pervasive one – so much so that we usually do not notice that this is precisely what we are all doing, all of the time.

This process is not, however, a purely internal one. Though it is a meaningful and sufficient encounter with self-narration that drives narrative therapy, the context in which these stories are told cannot go unnoticed. For it is the case that, just as external counter-stories are the key to liberation, so imprisoning, or problem, stories are often perpetuated and sustained by narratives that lie beyond the self. Therefore it is vital that the narrative therapist be aware of the context in which an individual's story takes place, of the philosophical and cultural ideas and beliefs that are generating and sustaining the problem. In short, the therapist is generating a narrative history of the self. In order to do this the narrative therapist considers a number of issues:

- What are the explicit background assumptions and presuppositions that enable this story to make sense for the individual?
- What worldview does the person hold?
- What implicit background assumptions made this story work? (Naturally, to understand a person at this level requires careful listening to their story long before any counter-narrative can be employed that may prove meaningful and sufficient.)
- What are the ideas that might explain how people are speaking and acting?
- What are some of the taken-for-granted ways of living and being that are assisting the life of the problem? (While many people can recognize their plight and their need of healing, not all will be able to distinguish the behaviour that is perpetuating their dilemma – partly because they see this as how they have always lived, so they ask 'Why change?'.)[88]

As we have already said, the post-industrialized self lives in a sea of stories. Though ultimately the story of the self is a personal one, the individual encounters a constant barrage of alternative or possible stories that may be partially or fully appropriated in order to generate a new story by which to live. To live in a post-industrialized context requires the individual to engage in a kind of conversation, or negotiation, between the stories that govern the self at any given moment and the alternative stories by which we might (re)narrate our lives. We are, therefore, always in the process of assessing our story alongside the narrative possibilities, or counter-stories, that challenge our own narration.

It might be helpful at this stage to return to an earlier observation: in postmodernity, all stories have equal and potential worth as narratives that may bring meaning and illumination to the life being lived. A story is legitimized by its usefulness, or de-legitimized if it proves meaningless. Postmoderns may well 'try on for size' any story they encounter that might prove meaningful and sufficient.

The narrative therapist has tapped into this relativism, using it to full advantage. Alan Parry and Robert Doan, for example, have begun to challenge the single, dominant story by inviting their clients to imagine and engage with the many possible stories that could be drawn from the family and friends of the individual. Their clients can begin to understand that there are other possible narratives by which they could story the self, because such stories already exist in reality for other people who know them. What this does is to call into question the very notion that there is one true story by which the self is forced to live. Once they grasp the profound yet simple concept that any story is just a story (however meaningful and sufficient it may or may not be), they are liberated from their current story and begin to re-narrate the self with fresh vigour. They 'invent stories of their own that serve the purpose of any narrative: to provide a framework of meaning and direction so that life can be lived intentionally'.[89] Through this liberation from a meaningless and insufficient dominating story the client can begin to change his or her own personal narrative in order to 'relate to self and others in life-enhancing, active ways, transcending the role of voiceless, passive, alienated victim'.[90]

It is the idea of the counter-story (or narrative) that lies at the heart of the methodology by which the narrative therapist seeks to bring a resolution to the conflict experienced by the self. According to narrative therapy, we are too often imprisoned by our stories, not liberated by them. They become prisons of meaninglessness that isolate and alienate the self. The narrative therapist has come to understand that, in order to address a storied-self meaningfully and sufficiently, one requires alternative narrations or counter-stories that question the power or validity of the story currently being employed to make sense of the self. But that may not be as straightforward as it sounds. People, it has been observed, can become extremely loyal, even to traumatic stories, if that is the only storied identity they have. The counter-narrative calls into question the validity of the current story being told. Metaphorically, or narratively speaking, the client must die to self by taking up the new, alternative narration of his or her life suggested by the therapist. 'Slowly [the therapist and the analysand] engage in co-authoring a new story. They construct a new identity.'[91]

Though this all sounds, and can indeed be, rather distressing, the methodology by which the therapist seeks to reconstruct the client's perception of self through narration is not a complex one. McLeod summarizes it thus:

> The main mode of operation of therapy is through the telling of stories. Clients or patients come in and, one way or another, tell their story and discover or construct new stories to tell. Therapists do not usually disclose stories of their own personal troubles, but instead offer their clients

more general, almost mythic, stories of how people change or what life can be like. Implicit in the therapist's story is an image of the 'good life'. Narratives of fulfilment, self-improvement and self-management are, of course, everywhere: movies, novels, advertising hoardings, glossy magazines. But what better way to seed these stories deep in the cultural soil than by giving people opportunity to acquire these stories through intimate conversations in which they can try out therapeutic narratives, versions of the good life, as templates for their own lives?[92]

While we may struggle to call them metanarratives, it becomes clear that the methodology employed in such analysis is to counter the less than helpful story, or stories, that dominate the client's world. Payne calls these 'counter-plots',[93] though this is simply a counter-story by another name. These are employed to break the cycle of self-justification, to cause the client to doubt the self that he or she has narrated to the 'outside world' and to construct an alternative story.

Clearly this encouragement to doubt the self narrated to the outside world has the potential to heal the chronically shamed, post-industrialized self, who typically narrates the self via the cover story, or the ideal-self. However, the challenge of narrative therapy to give up this false narrating means that the chronically shamed individual seeking therapeutic help must be open to change by giving up the current storied-self. Of course, the chronically shamed person may choose to narrate an ideal, false or cover story to the therapist. If this is the case, an alternative narration must not be forced upon the client. Instead, their story, as it is being told, must be listened to. Then, into the void of meaningless and insufficiency, the therapist begins to narrate other stories. Counter-stories, or narrative possibilities, are suggested that the client may choose to try or adopt for his or herself. Even without a 'real' self being present, there can be healing and transformation. For though the person being analysed may not let on as to their real self because of the wall of chronic shame that separates it from the outside world, the intimacy of conversation, the 'confusion' and recognition that occurs through this dialogue of story and counter-story leads the client, at the very least, to consider the potential the new narrative has for him or her to escape self-justification and to know and be known in a new and real(-self) way.

Thickening the story

Like all professions that work directly with the personal, social and relational self, narrative therapists engage people in all of their deep complexities. However, what they have begun to recognize is a tendency to over simplicity in narrating the meaninglessness and in-sufficiencies that traumatize the post-industrialized self. Instead of acknowledging and engaging the multiplicity of 'plot lines' that amalgamate into the one narrative of the self, the client, especially when faced with their own relational dysfunction, will typically opt for what narrative therapists call a 'thin description'. That is, they have a tendency to describe their plight and its causes in a rather superficial, monistic way – as do others, who may share in creating the context in which the self resides. Such 'thin' descriptions negate the possibility that their personal plight is almost certainly the result of a combination of factors, perhaps in the vain hope that isolating *the cause* will mean a simpler and more efficient resolution to the problem. The reality, however, is that a 'thin description' only serves to obscure other 'plot lines' and their toxic effect on the narrative consistency of the self. They leave the self isolated and disconnected from the realities that must be acknowledged if there is to be any possibility of healing.

Naturally, the narrative therapist would wish to argue that just as 'thin descriptions' of personal plight can support and sustain problems, alternative, counter-stories can reduce the influence of problems and create new possibilities for the self to narrate a fresh and ontologically consistent identity. Nonetheless, as one of the leading lights in the field of narrative therapy is at pains to point out, 'To be freed from the influence of problematic stories, it is not enough to simply re-author an alternative story. Narrative therapists are interested in finding ways in which these alternative stories can be "richly described".'[94]

These 'rich' or, as some prefer to describe them, 'thick' stories, are quite simply the opposite of a 'thin story' in that they are purposefully designed to account for and take seriously the complexities and the uniqueness of the individual's story. These stories deny that a human being is ever capable of narrating his or her plight through a singular and simple catch-all. They also deny that such monism can ever be meaningful and sufficient when dealing with relational beings. The narrative therapist is, therefore, interested in pursuing counter-narratives, in interweaving personal and corporate stories into a richness that is able to bring forth and thicken the story of the self so that the self's plight is dealt with meaningfully and sufficiently.

'Other' stories

Implicit in much of what has been stated and observed so far about narrative therapy has been the presence and the importance of the 'Other' in the formation of the post-industrialized self. Whether as a present, personal entity in relation with the self or as a sinister or helpful alternative story oozing from the cultural and philo-sophical context of the postmodern, the presence of the 'Other' is undeniable. However, despite its presence, seldom does the therapist explicitly suggest the 'Other' to the client – either as a mutual beneficiary of the healed relational self or as a priority consideration that may actually be a significant factor in helping to bring about ontological coherence. Indeed, though undeniably present, narratively speaking the 'Other' is anathema to the post-industrialized self because the ontological incoherence of the storied-self knows not to trust the stories of others.

The focus and emphasis of narrative therapy is always the self, first and last. Despite taking seriously the context in which it is at work, narrative therapy is the offspring of a more traditional psychotherapeutic methodology, 'that quintessential modernist creation, [which] placed the feelings and "needs" of the self ahead of obligations towards the other, because individuals felt particularly constrained by the demands of a moribund morality that insisted they despise themselves but love their fellow human beings'.[95] The result of this prioritizing of the self has been that the 'Other' has, in principle if not in reality, no ontological status in the narrative the post-industrialized self tells.

For stories to make sense and have cohesion, and so by implication for the identity of any given individual and their world not to implode, requires the 'Other'. It requires intimacy at least to the level of listening with intent to understand. To be human is to be accountable. Indeed, 'I am not only accountable. I am one who can always ask others for an account, who can put others to the question. I am part of their story, as they are part of mine.'[96] Tragically, without this narrative mutuality, both the 'Other' and the self are lost. No account is asked for, neither is it given, with the ultimate end that I cannot account for myself.

Clearly, any storied-self that contains relational dysfunction as a significant aspect of its plight cannot hope to find meaning and sufficiency in any narrative that precludes the 'Other', even if the ultimate purpose is to bring an ontological coherence to the self. As we shall discuss further, ontological coherence is something that is first and foremost discovered through prioritizing the 'Other' and not, as is the purpose of much psychotherapy, through privileging the self. 'Relation to the other is ultimately prior to [the self's] ontological relation to [his or herself] … [the] ethical relationship of love for the other stems from the fact that the self cannot survive by itself alone, cannot find meaning within its own being-in-the-world.'[97] With the absence of the 'Other', be it a person or community, there would be no one to listen to and challenge the self-deceiving narrative by which a person interprets the past, acts in the present and anticipates the future.

Even though they fear it to be so, the post-industrialized self knows that for the real-self to be known, for it to be shown up and so moved to a point of resolution, requires 'Other' storied realities. The self-deception typified by shame, the inconsistency between the ideal-self and the real-self, the contrast between our relationship towards others and the story we tell, all demonstrate clearly that 'self deception is recognized for what it is only when a person is called to some accounting by another person or by a community'.[98] Or, as Thiselton would wish to state, 'the identity of "the real self" emerges fully only *in relation to purposes which transcend the self*'.[99]

6. Narrative and Christian Soteriology

> What takes place in the collision between personal history and Christian narrative is that personal identity is illumined ... and one is called to a new form of life.[100]

With their use of counter-narratives to challenge the dominant story of the post-industrialized self, members of the therapeutic community are explicitly demonstrating what is implicitly taking place on a day-to-day basis in the lives of every individual within the towns and cities of the developed world. Through the medium of film, television, novels, magazines, radio, internet, advertising and personal encounter, stories are told, retold, agreed with, countered and subverted. All of these storied events, 'invite people to live in their world as the real world, even if it contrasts with the world of their hearers' current experience'.[101] The plurality of the post-industrialized world is a breeding ground for the stories and counter-stories that vie to be heard. These can then either be rejected, absorbed into self-narration or submitted to in a way that leads to what can only be described as a *conversion* – that is, 'a person's self-understanding or personal identity comes into question and one's personal history must be reworked, reinterpreted, and re-appropriated'.[102] That is not to say that conversion is a common event, nor one taken lightly by any given individual. Most people cling doggedly to the self that they have created and the world they wish that self to live in. But, from time to time, an alternative narrative so grips them that it has to be considered as a genuine alternative to the storied-self.

Given all that has been said so far, and even from the brief paragraph above, it would seem self-evident that the Christian faith is nothing more than (though vitally nothing less than) one story among an infinite number of other stories. For some, this is a worrying idea, and yet recognizing this fact is of far greater value than any attempt to rationalize the story of salvation, or formalize it into statements of fact or truthful propositions, which have little meaningful credibility in a postmodern context. As a story, on the other hand, it has the potential to encounter the post-industrialized self in ways that are meaningful and sufficient and which ultimately may lead to a conversion of the storied-self.

Though in the end it becomes clear that the Christian (meta)narrative makes unique claims upon truth, upon history, upon humanity and the origin and end of life, in its initial encounter with the self it should assert nothing more than the right to be heard, to be considered along with the polyphony of other voices, of other narratives that collide and conflict with any given individual or community. If it professes to do no more than any other narrative that is heard via therapy, novel, film or cyberspace – to live in the world they create as if it is the real world – then it is far more likely to be entertained as a possible alternative narration. Therefore, the Christian claim upon humanity is not given by reasoned account, by the logic of enlightened process. The atonement, conversion and salvation of a person are not given over to a formula reminiscent of scientific discovery. Conversion, rather, is the joining of one's personal story with the story of the Christian community and, by implication, with the story of God.

The story of salvation

In terms of a working definition, 'Soteriology is concerned with how humanity has moved or can move from a state of deprivation (however understood) to a state of release from deprivation … A Christian soteriology must show how this release occurs and what the role of the story of Jesus is in this release.'[103] This definition by Michael Root is clear and useful in that it demonstrates the rudiments of plot necessary to claim a narrative structure to Christian soteriology – an account of characters and events in a plot moving over time and space through conflict towards resolution. This echoes the same intent observed in the work of the narrative therapists and, more importantly, is recognizable to the storied-self, which understands the grammar of a world that is narrative-based.

More specifically, within the creation narrative humanity begins in self-deception and self-justification. Into this relational disruption comes a cover story and the attempt to hide the real-self, generating the ontological or narrative incoherence known only too well by the postmodern self. When we hear the narrative in this way we can understand that, primarily, human beings are to be held to account for that of which they are the authors. What is more, when the plight of humanity is narrated as a story that speaks of the loss of mutual, undistorted, unpolluted relationship, as the creation myth does, then we must look to narratives of *at-one-ment* to seek to resolve this, to reconcile human relations with each other and with the 'Other' – God. Indeed, to render the world in this fashion is to highlight the fact that *'at-one-ment ... is a metaphor which involves the goal of mutuality and the process of achieving it'.*[104]

Again, the concern here is not to speak of 'truth', if by that we mean the proving of something to be an undeniable fact or space/time event. What is far more important to our concern, and the plight of the postmodern, is whether we are encountering a story that is meaningful and sufficient. Therefore, we should feel comfortable with using terms such as 'myth' and 'story' when communicating soteriology, for by such means human beings express the meaning and significance of life, the mundane and the profound, the immanent and the transcendent.

Right from its very inception, the Christian church has worked as a community to generate narratives that explain meaningfully how the story of Jesus is sufficient for our salvation. In order for this to occur, not only was the story of Jesus' life and death taken seriously, but so too was the missional context into which that story was to be heard. Though reference was always made to the events that have taken place around the fields and towns of first-century Palestine, the way in which these stories were recalled always considered the cultural and philosophical surroundings in which they were told so that they would imbue the present with meaning and evoke hope in what was to come. What the early apostles and evangelists understood, and used to their advantage, was that stories have the most wonderful capacity to captivate a person entirely. However, if they hold no meaning for the place in which they are told, then their capacity to captivate dwindles.

What is being suggested here, and has been on a number of occasions already, is that at this juncture in history, our narratives, or more specifically the narratives we use to tell the story of atonement, have ceased to be captivating for the post-industrialized context in which the church finds itself. Therefore, in order to represent a narrative of atonement to the postmodern, the stories surrounding the life and death of Jesus of Nazareth must be *re-presented* in a form that is meaningful and sufficient to their plight as they tell it.

If we are willing to listen carefully and acceptingly to the reality of the story the post-industrialized self is telling, if we are humble enough to learn the power of the counter-story from the narrative therapists, then the Christian community should be in a better position to take seriously the contemporary plight of postmoderns and engage them meaningfully and sufficiently with a 'bespoke' version of the story of atonement rather than feeling that the stories and experiences of the post-modern self should conform to a reductionist version of sin and atonement that is held up as *the* story or model. As Stephen Pattison has lamented, 'a message such as "God loves you" could come to supplant and take precedent over the blunt, crude message "you are guilty, sinful, stained". This might enable people more easily to explore their sense of worth before having their worth-lessness and shame reinforced.'[105] After all, even taking Pauline interpretation into account, a biblical under-standing of atonement is concerned above all with the restoration of mutual, undistorted, unpolluted divine/human relationship, not with the appeasing of a God angered by the misdeeds of his creatures.

God is a storied-being

If the Christian claim to a personal God, to a personal Saviour, is to stand scrutiny then it must be seen that God, like his image-bearing creatures, is necessarily a storied-being. From his imagination God spoke, or 'narrated', into being all that there is. Rather than stating that God has a plan for creation, it is perhaps truer and more fruitfully engaging to suggest that God is telling a story, *the* story (if we can state that without falling back into the incredulous world of the metanarrative) into which our own personal story is narrated. Or perhaps it is more meaningful for the post-industrialized self to think in terms of the revelation that comes through God's own narration. This reveals not only the real identity of God but, as the individual comes to be convinced (or converted) by this story, it also reveals the real-self. God's own story brings forth the redeemed person, an ontology that is coherent – narratively meaningful and sufficient. In this way Christianity can claim to be the religion of the postmodern, 'because it is not founded on anything other than the performance of its story … a world of becoming, in which people are not fixed entities but life-narratives with a future.'[106]

To speak this way demonstrates the relational quality of narrative and its importance in shaping mutual, un-distorted, unpolluted relationships. Indeed, to be a storied-being is to be a relational being. The storied-God, whose own story is self-evidently prior to any human story, narrates his creation and his creatures from this singularity: 'In the beginning is the relation'.[107] There-fore, following logically from the idea of the eternal Trinity as existing in a *perichoretic* relationship – a relationship we are called to mimic and with which, therefore, the atonement must be concerned – God must *be* the divine ground, the limitless creative source of relational being. Consequently, we must understand that as his creatures it is redemptive for us to work towards forms of deeper mutuality within society, to seek mutual, undistorted unpolluted relating.

If for no other reason than the purpose of integrity, the Christian community needs to respond by communicating the story of salvation as an iconic story that reflects the undeniable, eternal reality that God is a relational, storied-being. Not only that, but our specific narratives of atonement must seek to emphasize, as a matter of priority, that Jesus' life and death were first and foremost about the healing and restoration of people lost in the meaninglessness that comes from living with an absence of mutual, undistorted, unpolluted relationships. Further, we must emphasize that the sacrifice was incarnational so that the atonement would take place 'in, with and under' human relationships.

> Looking upon the cross of Jesus Christ with its whole narrative treatment in Scripture centred in the morass and malaise of human relationships – the relationships of Jesus with his uncertain and vacillating disciples; the relationship of the priestly class to the charismatic religion of the Baptist and the prophetic religion of the Nazarene; the relationship of Rome to its subject states; and all the personal relationships encompassed in these greater categories – one wonders how, with this narrative as our window into the reality that biblical faith expounds, Christianity could ever have ended up with an ontology of substances and quantities and moralities and not of relations.[108]

Thickening our story

To state that the atonement is ultimately about the restoration of human/divine relations via the re-storying of the storied-self is but a starting point for our narratives of atonement. In describing the overall plight of humankind with such brevity, we need to be careful not to fall into the trap of producing a 'thin' story, which superficially covers over the complexities of the relational self. Nor should we produce a 'thin' story of atonement to deal with these complexities. In reality, the story of atonement needs to be rich and thick so that it can speak meaningfully and sufficiently to every storied-self it encounters: The lost need to be found. The socially excluded need to be welcomed. The sick need to be healed. The oppressed need to be liberated. The divided need to be reconciled. The chronically shamed need to become 'shame-less'. Ultimately, individual and communal need shape where the emphasis comes in the story of atonement.

Unfortunately, we have a tendency to over simplicity in narrating the meaninglessness and insufficiencies that traumatize people. Handling the plight of humankind in a monochrome fashion moves us towards simplistic stories of atonement. Such simplicity and 'sound bites' may help us to feel more comfortable in communicating the gospel to others, but in reality they fundamentally fail to communicate anything because they are, in themselves, meaningless and insufficient, 'thin descriptions' that deny the complexities and subtleties under which we all live. We are far more nuanced as human beings than is often allowed for in the stories we tell about the atonement.

Though the life and death of Jesus took place in a specific historical context, the *story* of atonement needs to be told in such a way that it is reincarnated meaningfully and sufficiently into every context it encounters. Our soteriologies need to take with great seriousness the human condition from which salvation is needed at each given point in history.

> If it is to the human condition that this work [the
> atonement] must be seen to speak, then this theology
> cannot and must not be allowed to substitute for concrete
> historical and contextual reflection a theoretical once-for-all
> preconception of what that human condition is. There is no
> 'human condition' if by that we mean something eternal
> and unchanging ...To be human is to be mutable, to change;
> it is to be historical; it is to be involved in flux.[109]

A story of atonement that orientates itself purely and
simply around the wrath of God, directed toward the self
for sins committed against a divine law, which is
absorbed by an innocent (Jesus), not only fails to map
onto the story of the post-industrialized 'sinless' self in
any meaningful way – it also fails to map onto significant
chunks of the New Testament. Indeed, the idea that the
Bible or the Christian community has traditionally had
one single, all-encompassing understanding of the story
of atonement is groundless. The Scriptures are replete
with stories that are full of metaphor, symbolism and
imagery that seek to address all manner of issues with
and without sacrifice. Even the New Testament
'struggles' (in a way that we apparently do not) to speak
singularly about the purpose for and meaning of Jesus'
death, with themes of justification, sacrifice, overcoming,
redemption and reconciliation interchanging with each
other. Therefore, to actively prefer one model over all
others is to work beyond the New Testament's own
witness about the life and death of Jesus.

At times the Christian community can be guilty of
believing that all people, at all times, inhabit the same
story that we do – a story about creation, fall, redemption
and re-creation, a story about sin and salvation. To put it
crudely, they do not. For they have their own stories
about themselves and the world around them. But this

assumption causes us to describe thinly the plight of the post-industrialized self, whose stories do not (in most cases cannot) begin with the concept of alienation from God. The postmodern narrative is about meaninglessness and the insufficiencies of relationships, about alienation from one another. Therefore, it is here that our stories of atonement, stories that need to be 'rich', or 'thick', must begin. These stories must be purposefully designed to account for and take seriously the complexities and the uniqueness of the individual's story. Therefore, the Christian community needs to work actively, creatively and imaginatively to furnish our stories of atonement with symbols and metaphors that more appropriately reflect the experience and plight of the postmodern self. In doing so, we will provide the grammar of faith, out of which they can re-narrate a new, authentic, ontologically coherent, 'converted' self.

We need to understand, then, that no one soteriological model is meaningful and sufficient for expressing all plights, all conflicts that need resolution. The story of salvation, therefore, is not a narrative with a single plot. The Christian community should be replete with a myriad of narratives from which to draw, all of which reach back to the transcendence of God, through the work of Christ (especially as defined by the cross) and on to a resolution. Like the endeavours of narrative therapy, these counter-stories, or narrative possibilities, are versions of the 'good life' that can be tried out as templates for our own lives to see how they fit.

Likewise, the post-industrialized storied-self is not a narrative with a single plot. The self is always under scrutiny, constantly shifting, relentlessly questioned; seldom, if ever, is it *at one* with itself. Constructing and reconstructing the storied-self is a journey that requires the full exercise of the whole person, including intellect, emotions and the spiritual conscience as well as those things that, even though suppressed into the realms of the unconscious, still haunt our lives.

As if to add weight to the earlier observation that atonement is a process, any conversion that these alternative, counter-stories might possibly bring will be one of a laboured progression, a journey rather than a sudden and radical decision. Stories need time to be told, life stories demand time to be lived. There may well be many significant encounters, conflicts and resolutions before the person is finally comfortable with narrating themselves from within the Christian story. Brueggemann renders the concept thus:

> Therapeutic talk …is characteristically heard only a little at a time, without any large sense of where one is going. Over time these little pieces may amount to an enormous challenge to one's ego-structure, and if one is blessed, they contain the hint of a massive reordering of one's self … [Christian] transformation is the slow, steady process of inviting each other into a counterstory about God, world, neighbor and self. This slow, steady process has as counterpoint the subversive process of unlearning and disengaging from a story we find no longer to be credible or adequate.[110]

Confessing a new story

Finally, however, it must be seen that no story of salvation can be meaningful or sufficient for the post-industrialized self unless the individual is able to confess and be atoned for – and as we saw from our discussion about chronic shame, that is precisely the incapability of the post-industrialized self. The fear of being exposed as an incoherent being has the very powerful effect of silencing the post-industrialized self so that he or she is unable to tell or confess who he or she really is.

Where sin is understood as pride, the egoistic concentration on self makes it relatively easy to extract a confession and so turn the key of salvation, if that is deemed necessary. Ironically, the proud want to tell you their stories, to confess all to all. They are shameless in every sense of the word. However, in such stories of salvation (where sin is thought of as pride) there is no space or understanding shown for people who have a poor sense of self or none at all – for those who suffer from chronic shame, to use our example. Though it sounds like an anathema, the 'sinless' person wants to hide. The chronically shamed do not want to confess because, from their very real perspective, that would be to live out a traumatic, destructive, shameful narrative that they fear being exposed.

Here, perhaps, the greatest lesson can be learned from the therapeutic community. As we have seen, when working with a client the psychotherapist typically narrates back not the patient's own story, but a 'myth'. Patients may not trust a direct account because they know that they themselves are not being truthful. What the therapist gives is a narrative possibility, a conflicting or counter-story – but one that can be recognized as bearable and conceivable, one which is yet to be lived, one which can be owned by the individual as their own truth, as their real-self. Here confession is possible when they have another story to which they can turn. The self is brought to account by the liberation of being able to author a counter-story to the narrative of shame that has held them captive.

If such ideas seem alien, unbiblical perhaps, then consider Joel Green and Mark Baker as they discuss the purpose of the evangelists in writing the Gospels:

Accepting [the writers'] invitations to enter their worlds
and to adopt a perspective from within those writings ...
[w]e come to appreciate how those writers sought to
communicate in language appropriate to their life
situations, while at the same time leaving ourselves open to
being challenged by their visions of reality and of the
purposes of God. This requires that we decentre our own
self-interests so as to be addressed by the text as 'other', to
allow it to engage us in creative discourse, to take the risk of
being shaped, indeed transformed in our encounter.[111]

The Christian community needs ways to allow those who
live in a world of shame to narrate fresh stories they
believe to be their own and so confess and be atoned for.
These must come not through testimony but through the
counter-stories of myth. We will argue later that the
intent of Christ, given at the Last Supper, and the
subsequent gospel narratives give such a myth a
narrative possibility to refigure our own world. For now
it is sufficient to say, along with Goldingay, that 'the
crucifixion story does things to the hearer that an
exposition of the doctrine of the atonement does not'.[112] It
is that story that is remembered and appropriated
continually among the Christian community at the
Eucharist. Here confession is done in safety because the
individual authors it himself or herself as he or she
reconstructs a new identity through the narrative of
atonement. In this way, confession may not be the public
announcement and revealing of the 'real' self so much as
'confessing' or 'narrating' a 'new' self, orientated around
the counter-narrative of the atoning life and death of
Jesus, which has become the dominant story for the self.
Confession is no longer the declaring of my shame to
others, but 'is that "moment" when the individual
believer ... is able to reconstruct personal identity by

means of what is acknowledged and recognized to be the truth about Jesus Christ',[113] and so by implication true of themselves.

III

The Intent of Jesus in the Gospels: Atonement as Ontological Coherence

7. Jesus Narrates His Intent:
A Story of Coherence

Jesus did not aim to be repudiated and killed; he aimed to charge with meaning his being repudiated and killed.[114]

With the biography of the 'sinless' post-industrialized self now told, and with it the importance and implications of narrative to construct and to counter the self, our attention must now be given over to the gospel accounts of Jesus. We need to read them as narratives of atonement: meaningful stories that can prove sufficient for the post-industrialized self, haunted by chronic shame, searching for the presence of mutual, undistorted, unpolluted relationship, longing for ontological coherence instead of personal and social alienation.

From the outset, it must be made clear that our goal is not the construction of a historical Jesus. This is an unnecessary distraction, for it is of no concern to the postmodern on their search for salvation. Like our therapeutic cousins we are merely seeking a narrative possibility that is bearable and conceivable, and one that can be owned by the individual as meaningful and sufficient. Indeed it has been suggested that those who seek a historical Jesus 'end with abstractions of their own making, in which the being of Jesus is not intrinsically connected with narrative occurrences, and such events therefore have no genuine significance'.[115] Or, to put it more crudely, the quest for the historical Jesus is not a quest for salvation but merely for fact.

Our goal here is to read the accounts as the gospel writers tell them, with particular emphasis on the Synoptic Gospels, and to consider their impact on the postmodern reader living in a 'sinless' society. For even if they are not 'literally descriptive of past events … They do, however, render the true identity of an actual person – Jesus of Nazareth … The gospels are not hypotheses but poetic and faithful narratives.'[116] As such they are ripe to be used as counter-stories of 'myth' to refigure the self and the world and bring the longed-for liberation of the postmodern self. As Garrett Green eloquently renders it, 'God offers himself to the imagination of his creatures by means of a "fictional" narrative – that is, one whose truth cannot be independently ascertained. In this way God "captures the imagination" of the faithful, the only kind of conquest that leaves them free.'[117]

In order to have some hope of a focused discussion, our attention will mainly be given over to the narrow time frame of the Passion Narrative, entering the story as Jesus and the disciples prepare to share what has become known as the Lord's Supper, or the Last Supper, and concluding at the cross of Calvary. While it is obvious that this is but a small window on the narrative of salvation, it needs to be acknowledged that it is not an insignificant one. For the Last Supper 'is an hour which cannot be transcended, and to which [we] must return time and again. For beyond it there is nothing, save the bringing to completion of what it freely inaugurates: dying.'[118]

For some, however, this idea of entering a story not at the beginning but towards the end may seem strange, even dangerous. After all, by doing this we can easily lose sight of the context and character development that allow the reader to make sense of what is going on in the narrative – vital and necessary aspects of plot, especially if the reader is to grasp the meaning and significance of the death of the main character. This is a fair and true observation, though there is perhaps enough in the Passion Narrative itself for the reader to grasp sufficiently who these characters are, their relationships to one another and the significance and urgency of the situation in which they find themselves. However, recognizing that we are about to enter the story at such a climactic stage, we will at times take excursions into the wider context in which this Passion Narrative is told, if for no other reason than to capture the imagination still further with the intent of Jesus as he tells the story around the table.

A story over supper

Even a cursory reading of the Gospels leaves the reader without any doubt that Jesus is an individual who is comfortable with narrating himself to others. On numerous occasions he speaks of his life and his, or his Father's, intentions for it. Indeed, at the beginning of Luke's rendering of the Jesus story we find him in the synagogue, narrating his intent through the words of another story, that of Isaiah and an exiled people (Luke 4:16ff.; cf. Isaiah 61). Such zeal must have been appealing to Judas Iscariot, one who was telling his own story of freedom fighting. But, like him, we must follow the

narrative of Jesus to its end to understand what precisely
he meant by this manifesto. For the Jesus who narrates
his intent at the Lord's Supper, who is crushed by fear in
the garden, who heals the 'enemy' there and calls his
disciples to lay down their swords, the Jesus who looks
into the eyes of those who crucify him and begs God to
forgive them, this Jesus looks and sounds entirely
different without interpretation – especially to one with
the zealous intent of Judas – to the 'storyteller' heard in
the synagogue. In fact, to the post-industrialized self,
Jesus may even appear as one who, like them, cannot
hold together the disparity between the ideal- and the
real-self.

Jesus gives numerous accounts about himself. In terms
of the intent he declares, and his subsequent actions that
are consistent with that account, however, none is more
striking to the reader, or to the disciples themselves, than
the story he tells at the Lord's Supper and the hours that
followed it.

> A group of friends gathers for a meal, each bringing some-
> thing to the table. They bring bread and wine. Their host
> brings himself. He has called them together, to share food
> and drink with one another. He tells them that in sharing
> the bread and drinking the cup they are sharing in him. He
> has given himself to them. He has given them his life.[119]

This is not the first meal that Jesus shares with his
disciples, or with others. Meals have been central in
communicating the heart of Jesus' ministry, literally and
symbolically, and in revealing his identity and purpose.
Ironically, given that at this particular meal he is about to
announce his impending execution to his friends, Jesus
typically shared meals as a way of concretizing his
message of 'good news' to the lost, to the marginalized

and excluded. Meals were moments of reconciliation, restorative encounters with isolated, alienated and fragmented people. Supper with Jesus was a *pre-at-one-ment* event, in more senses than one.

Despite the drama that surrounded these meals, here at the Last Supper, as never before, is intensity and immediacy that draws the reader. Jesus takes the familiar and reshapes it before the disciples and before the reader. He narrates to them the self-giving that is about to occur. He gives them bread and wine and tells them of his intent. Jesus' story of atonement is about to unfold – indeed, it is unfolding at that very moment in the Upper Room.

This is a story in which, along with his Father, Jesus is the author, the narrator and the central character. He is also the interpreter as he breaks the bread and passes the cup around. In these simple actions Jesus makes his intention clear. 'Not only are the loaves signs of Jesus' inclusive mission; now the loaf is his body, his very self … At this point the offering of bread-declared-body to the disciples becomes a vivid symbol of Jesus' death for others.'[120]

Jesus has instructed his friends on many occasions to devote their lives, as a matter of priority, to the service of others. Here, at this final meal with his friends, he tells them the story of his purpose for coming: not only to live in order to serve others, but also to face death, as we all must. This death, however, will be different. It will be for, and on behalf of, others. It will be an intended death, but not one born out of the inability to continue with a life lived in the absence of coherent ontology or lacking in mutual, undistorted, unpolluted relationship. This is not a *'putting to death of the self'*, either literally or meta-phorically, because Jesus is suffering an entire and absolute collapse of the self or because he fears that his real-self will be exposed. Paradoxically, his intent to die will ultimately prove his narrative and ontological coherence. His willingness to go to the cross at Golgotha will be in continuity with his story and due to the very fact that he lives with the constant *presence* of mutual, undistorted, unpolluted relationship.

Perhaps it is at this point that the narrative begins to open up and become a story of recognition and encounter for the post-industrialized self. For what Jesus is portraying is effectively his ideal-self; he is making known his desire to act in public. Postmoderns, especially those living a shame-driven existence, know this narrating of the ideal-self only too well. At this stage, however, it is unclear whether this Jesus suffers the same plight as the postmodern. Is this narration merely a cover story: an ideal-self to hide the shame of an incoherent ontology? The question that arises, and that is played out in the events to come, is whether this Jesus is able to do precisely what the post-industrialized self knows that he or she cannot – to hold together a narrative coherence between the ideal-self and the real-self. For Jesus' own story to be a narrative of atonement, it must contain a plot that is recognizable to the post-industrialized, 'sinless' self. It must also represent an alternative: a narrative possibility, a meaningful and sufficient counter-story that can be appropriated by the post-modern storied-self, isolated by chronic shame.

Once Jesus makes known his intent, once he declares publicly and narratively who his ideal-self is, the reader will begin to search the story avidly, to be assured that there is a narrative coherence between Jesus' intention and this subsequent action. If there is not, then the reader's suspicions will be aroused. Readers will doubt this ideal-self they are being told and turn away from the story, suspicious that what Jesus is narrating is merely a cover story to hide the fact that he can offer no hope of healing, restoration or reconciliation, for he is not even reconciled to himself. We must be careful not to abstract intent from action, 'as if ... the event of the crucifixion were anything without Jesus' resolve, or the resolve anything without the event in which it took concrete shape'.[121] This is fundamental in constructing a model of atonement for the post-industrialized self, for without the intent of Jesus the cross itself becomes nothing more than a hollow act. The reader is looking for the hope of ontological or narrative coherence and so for the possibility of living free of shame. The post-industrialized self is seeking a narrative identity that can hold together the ideal- and real-self without contradiction.

The reader is beckoned into the narrative by the hope that, perhaps, here is the narrative possibility of liberation from his or her own ontological incoherence, here is a counter-story with which to retell his or her own story in a coherent way without the fear of shame that comes through exposure. Jesus himself also beckons the reader, for without the willingness to walk the same path, to tell the same story, the reader will remain simply that – an onlooker into a storied reality. 'The cup Jesus offers to all his disciples is a share in his messianic suffering. Everyone who follows Jesus must be willing to drink the cup.'[122]

Jesus also gives a clue at the Lord's Supper as to his ability for self-consistency, his concern for 'Other' – human and divine. Through his storied-self Jesus does for the postmodern precisely what the therapist will not: he directs the lack of confidence in self-attention from our own private performance and self-justification to the subordination of the needs and interests of others. He brings the 'Other' into our story. Joel B. Green's comment on the story of the Lord's Supper is that

> We may understand Jesus as instructing his followers not
> only to continue sharing meals together, but to do so in a
> way that their fellowship meals recalled the significance of
> his own life and death in obedience to God on behalf of oth-
> ers. This recollection should have the effect of drawing forth
> responses reminiscent of Jesus' own table manners … his
> openness to outsiders, his comportment as a servant, his in-
> difference toward issues of status, honor, and the like – so
> that these features of his life would come to be embodied in
> the community.[123]

Jesus exemplifies this around the table, for here with him
is not only his 'betrayer' but also his friends who will all
desert him in his hour of need. His concern, however, is
not for himself but for them. Jesus maintains relationships up to the last, even in the most tragic of
circumstances. Indeed, his intent is to give up his life so
that living within mutual, undistorted, unpolluted self-
relating and 'Other-relating' may become a real possibility – even for the 'betrayer' who is dipping his hand
into the dish.

Of prodigals and adulterers

The Christian psychotherapist and counsellor Brian
Thorne, in his book *Person-centred Counselling and
Christian Spirituality*, writes of the daily experience of
meeting 'people who have no sense of their own identity
and who endure life as fragmented beings with no
awareness of the glory of being human'.[124] These are
people without worth, unlovable, if only in their own
eyes. Not infrequently they are chronically shamed,
weighed down by their inability to trust their own story
and the story of the 'Other', fearing exposure and dis-
respect. Thorne goes on to suggest in hopeful lament that

he, as a Christian and therapist, is to undertake to bring to such people an awareness of their own identity and to trust in their essential value and goodness. However, drawing his conversation close to ours he acknowledges that 'the obstacles in the way of such a pilgrimage (for it is a spiritual journey) are formidable and in the Passion narrative they are illuminated with chilling starkness'.[125]

Thorne reminds us that to purely look upon people as sinful creatures – proud, depraved, guilty before a divine creator – is to tell a 'thin' story of humankind not only of their relationship with God but even of their relationship with each other. This has important ramifications, because what we believe about the plight of humankind and God's response to us fundamentally affects how we in turn react to others and how they respond not only to us, but also to the stories of atonement we tell. The argument being put forward here is that the Gospels portray a Jesus who knew nothing of such thin descriptions of the plight of people, who never applied such ideas in his relating – either narratively or in praxis. The Gospels are full of lost, isolated, alienated and fragmented people: people without an awareness of the glory of being human. To such people Jesus brings his story of atonement – as we are charged to do. Naturally, this could be illustrated in numerous ways, but so as not to distract us for too long, one story and a single event will suffice.

In Luke 15, Jesus tells the story of the prodigal, or lost, son. Because this is a well-known story, the detail shall not detain us. What should detain us, however, given the plight of postmoderns and our search for meaningful and sufficient stories of atonement with which to engage them, is that here is a story from the very lips of Jesus that appears apathetic about concepts such as pride and guilt – though it is a story that could be read through these

lenses if we choose to do so. Also, culturally speaking, it
must be observed that the prodigal and his family knew
his 'sin' all too well, and that on his return there is an act
of confession offered – though this appears to be of little
concern to the elated father who is looking for restoration
and reconciliation without judgement.

For the post-industrialized self, the compassionate
response of the father turns this story not into an account
of pride and guilt or confessed sin that is forgiven.
Rather, it is a story about an isolated, alienated and fragmented person who is unconditionally welcomed by a
father just as he is. The story of the prodigal son is about
the creation of a valued-self through valuing that person.
The relational dysfunction that is so obviously present in
the narrative is absorbed by the father on the return of his
son, bringing the *at-one-ment* they both desire.

In a sense, by telling this story Jesus is narrating his
own self to those listening. As he will go on to state: 'I and
the Father are one' (John 10:30). The father's response to
the son and his desire, indeed his ability, to restore this
relationship, to make *at-one-ment* from relational disunity, is the intent of Jesus. This is his ideal-self. More
than that, it is his real-self – as the disciples and the
reader will come to understand.

In turning briefly to John's Gospel, we see Jesus live
out in reality the ideal he so eloquently narrates in the
story of the prodigal son. In the eighth chapter, a woman
caught in adultery is brought to Jesus. Certainly, in the
eyes of those gathered, she is a sinner. But again, as in the
story of the prodigal, sin and guilt, judgement and wrath
are not obvious dimensions of this narrative. The central
paradigm is the shame-destroying, person-affirming
inclusion of the woman without condemnation or concern for the 'sin' in which she has reputedly been
involved. Jesus is concerned to bring value and self-

worth to this woman. That is not the same as saying he ignored her moral offence – only that he chooses not to focus on it. Like the father of the prodigal, Jesus welcomes this fearful, isolated, alienated and fragmented woman, for this is the person he sees. In doing so, he personally absorbs the relational dysfunction that courses through this encounter on so many levels. Only then is the moral issue of offence against others or a divine law considered, for only now does she have the freedom at least to choose. Only after being included back into social relations does she move from being a pre-moral to a moral being (mirroring our earlier discussion on the chronically shamed being pre-moral). This brief encounter is turned from a story about the concerns of a self-righteous, baying mob into a pre-crucifixion narrative of atonement.

Gethsemane: The testing of Jesus' intent

At this stage in the narrative the reader is in no doubt as to the intention of Jesus. But as the full implication of that intent is realized and as the disciples begin to fail him – unable to hold to their bold claims that they can indeed drink the cup that Jesus is about to drink and suffer as he will – doubts are raised as to Jesus' own ability to hold together that intent with public action. In this way the garden at Gethsemane becomes a garden of fear – not only for Jesus, but also for the reader. There is a narrative tension beginning to build. For if Jesus is to fail here then there will be no cross, there will be no consistency between Jesus' ideal-self and his real-self, and so by implication there will be no hope of liberation and reconciliation for the post-industrialized self crushed by chronic shame. Loughlin may well be right to say that

'Jesus is most himself in his resolve to go to Jerusalem, to drink the cup his Father gives him.'[126] But to the reader he is more than that. 'Death as such, even the violent and truly horrible death of crucifixion, is not the primary issue here ... The fundamental question ... is whether as God's deputy he will take the final step toward the world ... whether as *our* deputy he will say yes to our creaturely condition.'[127] His entire ontology, his believability as a human being of self-consistency and narrative coherence (counter to the shame that resides in those that look to this story for the possibility of alternative narration), is dependent on Jesus' ability at this moment in the plot to say yes to his ideal-self.

It is here in the Passion Narrative that the clue as to self-consistency that was hinted at during the Supper – his concern for 'Other' – is brought into full view. 'The prayer-agony on the Mount of Olives has as its unique object a saying "Yes" to the will of the Father.'[128] Gethsemane has become the place where Jesus wrestles with his ideal-self (the one whose intent it is to go to the cross for all) and the possibility that his real-self would seek to walk away from the garden and so, by this act, from others and from God. Jesus can hold these two together and so have coherence and consistency in his story, despite the fact that there is the temptation to dispense with a self that is orientated to an intimacy based upon prioritizing the 'Other' and to live as the reader does – in self-seeking and self-justification.

In Jesus we see a person rooted in a mutual relationship with God, who is his source and resource for relational engagement. It is this mutuality in relating that Jesus desires for his friends. Jesus' ontological ability to sustain mutuality in his relationships expresses something vital not only about his connection to God, but it is also 'the key to Jesus' developing personality, self-consciousness and relationship with the men, women and children of his life, as well as the drive to his understanding of his mission to save the world – in fact to the central question of the meaning of salvation.'[129]

Later in the New Testament, the writer of Hebrews will make the comforting claim that 'we do not have a high priest who is unable to sympathize with our weaknesses, but we have one who has been tempted in every way, just as we are – yet was without sin' (Hebrews 4:15). This being without sin is certainly Jesus' ability not to act contrary to the will of his Father (God). A more significant, more meaningful and sufficient understanding, however, is to read this 'without sin' not negatively but positively, in the light of Jesus' own story and actions: it is the presence of a mutual, undistorted, unpolluted relationship with himself, with others and with God the Father. If we are to speak at all of the 'sinless' having 'sin', then we must do so as we gaze at this 'icon' of personal authenticity and relational coherence. For to do so allows us to understand that we are 'sinners' – not because we err in relation to a divine imperative, but because our lives are lived with the *absence* of the kind of relatedness modelled by Jesus.

For the encouragement of the reader, Jesus, in the face of agony and temptation not to pursue his intent, acknowledges the fact that to deny the cross would be to deny others their freedom, to deny God's story, which is prior to Jesus' own narration of himself, as well as to deny himself ontological coherence. 'He invites this kind of death because of a conviction that it is necessary … [but] Jesus still fears it.'[130] The 'Yes' to God's will is therefore not portrayed as a submissive act that somehow suppresses the self, but as an act that allows the realization of the real-self. It is a 'Yes' to the trust of another. Self-contradiction is only held at bay by the submission, the inclusion of the other, into the storied-self.

So it is that Jesus is resolved to act out his intent, to demonstrate by the cruellest death that here is a human being who will not walk the way of self-contradiction but will embrace all that his ideal-self, and God, wills. Read in this way, the arrest of Jesus is not the culmination of the betrayal of Judas and the inability of the other disciples to be faithful in keeping watch, but simply, 'the enactment of the same transition which had taken place, just before this, on the inner plane'.[131] The next time the disciples will see this Jesus will be at the acme of his self-giving – dying for others upon a cross.

8. Judas and the Disciples: Narrative Incoherence

> The story of Judas forms a narrative frame around the gospel account of the Last Supper.[132]

Running counter to Jesus' story is the intent of another – Judas. Although what we want to do here is to focus on Judas' story in the context of the wider narrative as a paradigm the post-industrialized self may well recognize, there are obvious risks in doing so. Judas is, after all, the despised betrayer of history, and so we must ask the question: who could possibly wish to associate themselves with such a character? As we shall see, however, when Judas' story is handled in a more sympathetic way the reader becomes acquainted with one who is self-despising long before others despise him. Judas is also a victim in this story. He is the self-betrayed as much as he is the betrayer. Indeed, as we shall see, he also suffers the tragedy of being betrayed by those close to him even as he 'plots' to hand Jesus over to the authorities.

Without doubt Judas is a tragic figure, like so many of us. However, if we allow his story to be told without adding the viperous traditions of interpretation, then he is perhaps not as evil as we would wish to believe. For while the Synoptic Gospels focus our attention on that infamous kiss, John's account prefers to emphasize Jesus' personal indication that he is the one the guards have come looking for (John 18:4–5, 7–8). Perhaps Jesus was trying to pre-empt the inevitable kiss, not wishing a disciple he loved to suffer any more confusion and anguish than was already in his heart. Or possibly Jesus is simply emphasizing that this is Gethsemane, the place where his own suffering begins, the prelude to the cross and the bringing of *at-one-ment* to those who lack it – not a place for continuing the tragedies of this world (Luke 22:49; John 18:10,11). At the very least, when speaking of Judas we would do well to recall the compassionate and heart-rending greeting given to him by Jesus, even as he places his kiss: 'My friend' (Matthew 26:50).

But the purpose here is not to defend Judas but to seek a foil, a character that the reader may recognize as being like him or herself and with whom he or she may empathize. That said, for obvious reasons it would be hard to suggest that Judas *was* suffering from chronic shame as the post-industrialized self would understand it. However, narratively speaking, Judas' intent, actions and response to 'Others' certainly show the symptoms of chronic shame, if not the full-blown *dis-ease*. As Stephen Pattison writes,

> Some shamed people lack a sense of personal worth and value. This means that they may act compliantly and in such a way as to attract approval from outside themselves rather than being concerned to do the right thing or what is best for others. The need to be acceptable may also cause shamed people to lie or be dishonest.[133]

We do not need to spell out how these symptoms of chronic shame relate to the story of Judas. It is enough to

say that, by looking for and emphasizing family resemblances such as these within the narrative, the story
of Judas can bridge the divide between historical,
cultural and psychological contexts and so become
meaningful in a way that a purely historical-critical
hermeneutic cannot, insightful as this method can be.

Despite our traditions leaving us with the sense that
we know all too well who this person is, in reality the
Gospels do not give us a full character development of
Judas. This is not to suggest, however, that we are to treat
Judas as a blank canvas onto which we can read any
psychological, emotional or behavioural traits we wish.
We know who Judas is and we know what he does.
Nevertheless, we are left unsure why it is that Judas acts
in the way he does, even with the usual suspects of
money, power and the devil lurking in the shadows.
Certainly, Judas was no puppet. Just as Jesus wrestled
with the divine plan in the garden of Gethsemane,
questioning and doubting his ability to drink the cup
poured out for him, so Judas also felt the anguish of that
most cherished of human gifts – free will.

Of course, a quest for the historical Judas may well
build a reasonable cultural and personal profile of the
man, shedding some light on the question 'Why?'. Such
knowledge, however, may only serve to keep Judas
anchored to the page, trapped in the first century, when
our need is for a meaningful engagement with a counter-
story that can purge the ontologically incoherent and
chronically shamed post-industrialized self of the
twenty-first century. The reader of the story, therefore,
needs the freedom to impress their emotion, intuition
and imagination onto the narrative, so that it may
become meaningful and sufficient for them, even if the
Christian community may tremble at the relativism this

implies. However, as we suggested earlier, if we are satisfied that our story is *the* story, interpreting without remainder the plight of humankind and the path to reconciliation and restoration, then we must allow the narrative equal freedom to engage, question and interpret the reader. For though it may be naïve to think that such a narrative could only have one meaning over time and space, it is unlikely to allow itself to be 'bullied' into confessing a meaning that is contrary to its ultimate purpose.

To read Judas through the eyes of the post-industrialized self is to gaze into a narrative mirror. Here is one who, like the postmodern, lacks ontological coherence. We may not be privy to his private thoughts, to his real-self, but we are drawn to one whose life so obviously becomes meaningless in the hours after the betrayal in the garden of Gethsemane. We know there is disparity between his intent and the actual events that took place (Matthew 27:1–5). Judas experienced the total and utter collapse of his personal narrative – psychologically, socially and spiritually. In sheer desperation, he takes what he believes to be his only option – suicide.

Here was a man divided from himself and from all 'Others'. He was incapable of maintaining his own self-coherence and inner-relatedness, let alone being of sufficient social ability and worth to relate to others without dysfunction. There is little doubt he would have felt polluted and stained, deficient as a human being. The post-industrialized self reads the story of Judas and recognizes someone traumatized by the *dis-ease* of chronic shame. So, with that in mind, we turn to the detail in the hope that this desperate story may also carry the seeds of *at-one-ment* among its ruins.

Judas 'frames' Jesus

There is paradox in the encounter between Jesus and Judas on a number of levels. For a start, even though some accounts allow us the narrative foresight of knowing who the 'betrayer' will be, the rest of the story is typically one of fellowship and friendship between Jesus and Judas. Indeed, Donald Senior comments that 'the whole thrust of the scene [the dipping of the bread at a meal of fellowship and kinship] is to interpret Judas' act as a betrayal of friendship'.[134] Judas is still one of the twelve and is present at the most intimate moment of Jesus' ministry. Yet, despite this friendship, here is one who struggles to maintain mutuality in relating. While it is perhaps unfair to suggest that Judas has no concern for his friends, he typifies the post-industrialized self in that his true agenda in relating is always intimacy for himself. It is soon to be revealed to the disciples, and to the reader, that the intimacy Judas craves is purely for his own self-satisfaction and that others are expendable as he searches to hold together his ideal- or real-self.

Though Jesus' own version of events is that he gives himself up, this does not diminish the fact that Judas also 'gives' Jesus up by betraying him. Even when portrayed as being used by the authorities or even as a pawn of Satan, 'Judas' destined role in the drama of salvation does not reduce him to a helpless marionette; he chooses betrayal'.[135]

This demythologizing of the event allows readers to be drawn into the narrative, raising questions about their own story, perhaps taking them in a direction that is unfamiliar to them – are they not also the betrayer in their own relationships and search for intimacy? This narrative ambiguity is compounded, particularly in

Luke's rendering of the scene, for 'the Third Evangelist shows no interest in naming the betrayer ... Luke leaves the apostles to discuss among themselves who it might be; this is troubling, since it suggests that any one of them is capable of breaking with Jesus'.[136]

The reader is slowly brought to an awareness that Jesus is the only one around the table who is not self-seeking or self-justifying in his intimacy – he is the only one who can be trusted. Only he has a coherent ontology, a story that holds together his ideal- and real-self. Only he relates without the distortions so common to us all. He is being revealed as the victim who, unlike the post-industrialized self, does not shun the 'Other'. Rather, he absorbs the dysfunction of human relating, especially that of his immediate companions, and forgives them by breaking bread rather than his fellowship with them. Confronted with such a scenario, the reader 'cannot avoid repeating the anguished question of the apostles: "Is it I?" The power of the passion drama lies precisely in such invitations for the reader to participate.'[137] But the question calls to mind not only the 'betrayal' of the one being revealed within the narrative, but also the reader's day-to-day relations.

Other betrayals

Once revealed, Judas slips away into the darkness of isolation brought on by his inability to maintain these personal relationships. The remaining disciples turn from him in disgust. It would appear that, for some un-known reason, Judas is determined to destroy the intimacy, friendship and love shown to him by Jesus. Yet the complexities of personal relating should not allow us to think that this is a 'thin' story in which only one person is responsible for the absence of mutual, undistorted, unpolluted relationship within this friendship group.

Were the disciples so ignorant, so unable to read the signs, that they knew nothing of the enormity of what was happening around them? Surely Judas was not hurrying away to replenish food for the table. Surely the disciples could feel the distress that must have come over Jesus as he watched one of his closest friends depart. Still, for whatever reason, there was no attempt to stop him, no one willing to inquire after his welfare He was left to his own devices, to disappear from their lives into the darkness. With the exception of Jesus, Judas is betrayed by the inability of his friends to consider the 'Other' rather than themselves. 'Judas is made the receptacle for all the negative feelings in the group … left alone … there is nothing that can impede his descent … therefore, [Judas] becomes the betrayer and sets out to destroy the love from which he now feels alienated.'[138]

To add insult to injury, the disciples are revealed as having no concern for the events that Jesus has told them will unfold. Peter's own denial of Jesus now becomes part of the story. Peter has to endure that which the chronically-shamed fear most – exposure of the real-self – though it is not Peter who acts to reveal this in some kind of confession. Surprisingly for the reader, it is Jesus who seeks to expose Peter's real-self, turning to say to him and all present in that Upper Room: 'This is your story, Peter, this is who you are and what you will do. This Peter is your real-self.' Understandably, Peter reaches for a cover story, especially given the rather public nature in which he is exposed, 'denying' that this is who he is. However, as the reader is soon to discover, he too lacks coherence in his personal narrative and reveals his real-self over and above the ideal he narrates to Jesus and the other disciples (see Matthew 26:31ff., 69–70).

Though it is of little comfort, neither is Peter alone in his 'betrayal'. In the Lukan account the disciples slip en masse into their own 'betrayal' of what Jesus is doing among them and for them. Even as the door closes behind Judas, an argument breaks out as to who is the closest to Jesus, the most loyal friend, the truest companion and therefore the most important in the kingdom he has come to establish (Luke 22:24). Once again, those close to Jesus are revealed as self-serving, they are, like Judas, their own cause. While this argument reveals a concern for 'Other' in that it looks beyond the present to a new reality, it still suggests that the element of 'Other' is missing from the self-narration of the disciples. For as Vincent Brümmer points out, 'If we love heaven rather than God, then our efforts are directed toward our own interests'.[139]

Out into the dark veil

Though some New Testament scholars have understood Judas' death as an act of atonement,[140] for obvious reasons it cannot be understood this way in the strictest sense of the word, nor can it be understood metaphorically. Indeed, Judas kills himself because he is not 'at one' with himself, or with Jesus, or with the other disciples. Far from leading to *at-one-ment*, his death, in reality, robs all of the opportunity for reconciliation. This, however, does not answer the question: why did Judas commit suicide? Did he act out of a sense of honour, as an act of repentance perhaps (a fruitful avenue not pursued here), or in order to hide the lost, alienated and desperate self?

'When someone complains … that his or her life is meaningless, he or she is often complaining that the narrative of their life has become unintelligible to them, that it lacks any point, any movement towards a climax or a telos.'[141] We need look no further than Judas to find a paradigm for such dysfunction, for here is one without any sense of coherence in his personal narrative. At this point in his life he must have been feeling the exact same emotions experienced by the post-industrialized self, lost as he was in the darkness of chronic shame: excluded, inferior, defiled, polluted and polluting. He embodied the anti-ideal.

> When Judas leaves the Upper Room he is in hell [because of the incoherence of his own narrative which has caused to him to reject others and so reject himself] and remains there until the end of his earthly life. It is a grim thought that he may have been driven there by lack of love and under-standing on the part of the other disciples and that the love of Jesus for him was ultimately powerless in the face of the indifference or even hostility of the others.[142]

Even with Judas' desperation so eloquently suggested, there is perhaps a question that hangs over this narrative: why did Judas not attempt to atone for the 'wrong' he had done? A simple confession would surely have remedied even this tragic breakdown of intimacy and friendship. Again we must be careful not to apply a 'thin' description to the complexities of this story, or indeed the complexities of all relating. From within the narrative itself, even if Judas had had the desire or the emotional and psychological well-being to attempt to express himself to Jesus in the form of a 'confession', it is rather difficult to imagine, given the chain of events in place, just how he would have managed this. More signifi-cantly for the postmodern reader, tacitly aware of his or her chronic shame, confession would be an unthinkable option. For, as we know from our earlier discussions about the post-industrialized self, confession would be an act that would expose the real-self and relive the moment of shame. That Judas would isolate and exclude himself from this intimate group of friends, even taking his own life, makes far more sense to the post-industrialized self reading this story. For the post-industrialized self, too, would seek the complete antithesis to confession and exposure: blocking out the other, hiding the self, or even pulling *the* dark veil over the soul.

On to Golgotha

As we saw above, 'the Supper is set in a tension of solidarity and betrayal'.[143] Jesus is left alone to face the death he announced to his disciples. Although he has clearly narrated that what he is about to go through is for them and for others, they can only muster commitment to themselves. But there is hope. For the biblical account does not portray what they do as a deliberate act but rather as an ontological failing, something that is beyond them in their present human condition. 'Unlike the opponents, the disciples do not destroy Jesus to save their lives. They are not against him. They fail at being *for* him.'[144] So it is for the post-industrialized self, who is not *against* those with whom he or she seeks, indeed craves, intimacy. Yet he or she fails at being *for* the 'Other'. The desire to self-serve blinds the individual to the possibility and the benefits of serving others and, in that denial of serving and concern, they become self-justifying.

> Whereas Judas [kills] himself … Jesus will not fall victim to self-rejection. He will survive the emotional bludgeoning because he is at one with himself, or as he himself is recorded as saying, 'The Father and I are one.' The intimate group destroys Judas but even when it does its worst it cannot undermine the trust of Jesus in his own identity.[145]

Here, as Judas and the disciples frame Jesus' story of narrative coherence, we see mirrored the 'sin' of the post-industrialized self – the absence of mutual, undistorted, unpolluted relating. For we disrupt our fellowship with the 'Other' by trying to pursue our own interests in the stories we tell. In this way 'sin' becomes not a state of corruption, nor guilt to be wiped out, but alienation from the 'Other', requiring reconciliation. Jesus portrays this reconciliation in his intent and his action. Despite the inability of Jesus' companions to relate without dysfunction, Jesus does not withdraw from the 'Other', not even Judas, nor does he in any way give up his intent. For in Jesus' story, at least, there is the possibility of reconciliation – even after these acts of betrayal.

9. From 'Death' to Life: The Hope of Ontological Coherence

> To be fully human means to embody a vulnerability that may well court and invite a wounding unto death.[146]

Given the metaphorical and literal place of death in the story of the post-industrialized self – and its role in cutting off the chronically shamed, incoherent, storied-self from every meaningful and potentially healing relationship – it would seem almost paradoxical, even oxymoronic, for Jesus to pursue such an end as a way of bringing *at-one-ment* to a relationally suffering humanity. And yet that is precisely where this story takes us.

> A Creator who through loving and liberating participation in the creaturely condition would redeem it 'must' (once the decision has been taken) follow the creature through that non-being 'toward' which all creaturely beings move – that end, let us already note, which does not come only at the end of life, but is deeply embedded in human consciousness all the way through . . . The divine love that is ready to suffer birth in human form 'must' follow through, if it is really love for creatures, for us. It 'must' suffer life, not only birth; it 'must' suffer death, too.[147]

According to Jesus' own story and the narratives that surround it, death is, at one and the same time, that which ultimately denies people the possibility of the *presence* of mutual, undistorted, unpolluted relationship and the means by which such relating is made possible. We will recall from our earlier discussions about soteriology that it is through Jesus' death that humanity has moved, or can move, from a state of relational deprivation to a state of release from that deprivation. Given such complexities, we should not assume that we are about to enter a 'thin' story. Indeed, in many ways the movement from deprivation to *at-one-ment* is a mystery: a hidden, imperceptible, almost intuitive re-storying of the self as it encounters the narrative and makes it meaningful and sufficient for its plight. Therefore, to try and account for *how* the death of Jesus reconciles the isolated, alienated self to the 'Other' – for that is what atonement is – can only ever be a personal interpretation that may or may not be recognizable as a narrative of atonement to others. After all, no two encounters with the storied-Jesus are the same. Certainly, it would be foolish to suggest that here is *the* grammar of the story that all will find meaningful and sufficient and by which the post-industrialized self will be liberated from chronic shame and ontological incoherence. What follows is no formulaic answer to the plight of the postmodern but a story that in its telling is heard, and therefore becomes, a narrative possibility that may bring *at-one-ment*, just as it tells of one who is himself, ontologically, narratively and relationally, 'at-one' – even in his dying.

A purposeful giving-up

In stark contrast to the suicide of Judas, Jesus' death is not a hopeless giving up of a life by one who could see no way back from his isolation. It is not a declaration of narrative incoherence with its inevitable meaningless-ness, nor is the death of Jesus brought about because he cannot bear the absence of mutual, unpolluted, undistorted relating. Indeed, Jesus' death is the counter-story to the narrative incoherence we find in the story of Judas, and it is also the counter-story to the narrative incoherence of the post-industrialized self. It is an embracing of death, a going to that place which all human beings must go. This is not because death in and of itself is something to be feared, but because it represents metaphorically, and is in reality, a place of isolation, alienation and meaninglessness. To die in the absence of mutual, unpolluted, undistorted relating is the most inhuman, insufficient place one can be in, for it is a denial of the authenticity in which we were created as image bearers of *the* relational being – God. If we take our cue from Brian Thorne,[148] however, it must be seen that the post-industrialized self flees from the awesome, unbelievable reality that to be fully human is to share in the divine nature: the ability to live in narrative and ontological coherence and to *be* in the presence of mutual, undistorted, unpolluted relating. Perhaps this is why so many of us distance ourselves from Jesus as if he is not really one of us at all. But he is. He, like us, is a storied-being. Therefore, as our narrative representative, he dies to show us what it means to accept our true natures: 'We are gods and yet we shall die like men' (Psalm 82).

'The cross of Jesus Christ represents simultaneously a high estimate of the human creature, a grave realism concerning human alienation, and the compassionate determination of God to bring humankind to the realiza-tion of its potentiality for authenticity.'[149] In this context, Jesus' death is a purposeful act of self-giving, fully in harmony with the intent of his storied-self. He is not passively killed, like an animal sacrifice – he is active – he gives up his life. This is not the story of an execution, nor the story of those who put him to death – it is Jesus' story. More than that, it is the story of one who desires that we, too, would live and die with the same ontological and narrative coherence that he himself knows.

That said, it is not a story that is always easy to read. For while Jesus' 'likeness' to ourselves serves to draw the reader ever deeper into the story, this likeness also heightens the narrative tension that began in the turmoil of Gethsemane. So it is that, despite the fact that Jesus' death is to be read as the pinnacle of his purposeful intent, the chronically shamed, narratively incoherent self cannot help but feel that it is also a further testing of Jesus' resolve to act in accordance with his ideal-self, so starkly narrated at his last supper with the disciples. The hours in Gethsemane are proven not to be a once in a lifetime occurrence. Once again a question mark hangs over the story of Jesus and his ability to live a narratively coherent life. *At-one-ment* is, as we have observed, a process – a story with many 'acts'. So it is that 'on the cross, Jesus exemplifies his own counsel by resisting the temptation to do as the passer-by, the religious leaders, and two robbers call on him to do, namely, to save himself'.[150] For to come down from the cross would serve to save neither others nor himself. Indeed, to do so would be to break with his storied-self, to destroy the narrative coherence of his personal story and with it the possibility of *at-one-ment* for all.

This tension in the narrative lasts until the end, focusing the reader upon the importance of Jesus' final exhalation and intake of breath. 'At the decisive moment, Luke replaces the ultimate *paradōsis* by the Father, namely, the Son's cry of abandonment on the cross, with the ultimate *paradōsis* by the Son, who gives over his spirit into the Father's hand.'[151] So it is that even though Jesus tastes God-abandonment, the effective severing of his narrated-self by the Father, it is Jesus, according to Luke at least, who continues on as if the severance had never occurred: 'Father, into your hands I commit my spirit' (Luke 23:46). Jesus' death takes place without contradiction to his intent and in the trust that God is able to continue to narrate his story beyond death. However, despite this apparent abandonment by God, Jesus is unwilling to go the same route. Almost in act of 'forgiveness' toward his Father, Jesus maintains his relationship by offering the gift of his life to the 'Other', setting his death in the context of a person-to-person relationship.

In spite of the ever-present narrative tensions and the uncertainties of a resolution, in the story of Jesus the cross is the most compelling symbol of his commitment to give his life for 'Others'. The cross is the public reality of the private symbolism of the Upper Room. The bread broken at the Lord's Supper is now brutally present on a hill named Golgotha. But it has to be so, for narration of intent without significant action leaves all concerned without the hope of liberation. The breaking of bread is an act insufficient to move not only Jesus but, more importantly, the disciples and the onlookers (including, now, the reader), into a place without contradiction – of coherence, where there is mutual, undistorted, un-polluted relating. The intent of the ideal-self must be acted out in the physical reality of the real-self, for 'the body is at once – and under different descriptions – the link between the self and the public world and the intentional self in, or enacted in, the public world'.[152] Therefore, as Jesus stretches his arms out along the crossbeam, he is, at one and the same time, symbolically holding together his own story and 'exposing' his real-self without fear of incoherence or the malady of chronic shame that haunts the postmodern self; for he is, at this moment, 'at-one'.

Absorbing the absence

Described briefly, the atonement is an act of love that restores the relationship between humanity and God by removing all boundaries that separate us – including death. It is the making possible the *presence* of mutual, undistorted, unpolluted relating between the individual and the 'Other', for to be 'at-one' in this way is to be human as God intended.

In encountering the storied reality of Jesus we become aware of the power of 'Other-focused' living to bring about the *at-one-ment* craved by the post-industrialized self. However, time and again it has been necessary to affirm that our plight is that we live with an *absence* of mutual, undistorted, unpolluted relating. The boundary for the postmodern self, living in a 'sinless' society, is that due to an ontological incoherence and varying degrees of chronic shame, we are unable to follow Jesus into this 'Other-focused' living. For this boundary to be removed, the incoherent self has to be removed – either onto-logically, through bringing about a narrative coherence, or physically through death. Postmoderns live with this impasse and search avidly the stories around them, in the hope of finding a counter-story, a narrative possibility that may bring them to a resolution: shameless, ontological coherence. Jesus' story is full of narrative possibility, but it needs to be told in such a way that it can become the meaningful and sufficient counter-story for which the postmodern is searching.

If one requires a symbol, a metaphor that could sum up entirely the absence of mutual, undistorted, unpolluted relating, then we need look no further than the cross on which Jesus died. For this is *the* death outside society. Jesus, like the scapegoat of the Old Testament narratives of atonement, was sent outside the city walls, into the wilderness, away from community. He was isolated, excluded, tormented, abandoned and alienated. He was in a place of pollution (literally as well as metaphorically) from which he could not return. Even before his last breath, Jesus was 'dead' because he was cut off from human relating, suspended between heaven and earth in a place of non-meaning. This relational dehumanizing, more than physical pain and suffering, was the purpose of crucifixion. Therefore, as if we need reminding, Jesus' final hour has come. However, he has not died a passive death, as if this were sufficient to communicate his last act of intent. Rather, his concluding moments have become a clarification of all that has preceded. 'The ultimate renunciation occurs when he gives up his own life … His death is the final act in a life of service and manifests his refusal to oppress others to save himself.'[153] Even in death, Jesus absorbs the relational dysfunction of others.

To frame Jesus once more with the narrative of Judas: both Judas and Jesus die on trees away from human relating. Though both, it may be suggested, are 'offerings', only one is efficacious. Judas does not restore his own relationships, or those of anyone else, through his death because he dies in the absence of mutual, undistorted, unpolluted relating. His death represents his life, and the life of all who suffer the same absence – and that includes the postmodern self. Those who suffer shame are metaphorically and literally absent from normal human relating. They too 'die outside the city walls', in a place of non-meaning and non-being:

Groups and individuals who fall into a state of long-term toxic unwantedness, abomination and abjection find themselves the objects of inarticulate stigma and rejection to others and often themselves. They inhabit a state which is beyond words, outside humanly defined and recognized reality, in a wasteland of uncleanness … any person or group that is habitually shamed will be dehumanized. Shame is an important marker of the bounds of human community and belonging. Those who live beyond the shame boundary inhabit the realm of the unclean and inhuman.[154]

Jesus' death, however, takes on this non-relatedness, this non-being, by making way for the possibility of a restoration of relationship – resurrection, even. Jesus' story makes us privy to the fact that in human relating the initiative lies with the man who is narratively free, ontologically coherent and relationally sufficient. For as the individuals and communities who encountered Jesus begin to reject the one who is fully 'at-one' with himself and with the 'Other', they in fact show themselves to be the ones who live with relational absence.

The cross, however, is not a place of judgement for the inadequacies and insufficiencies of human relating. Indeed, it is a place of acceptance, of embracing the human condition. Atonement is the presence of the 'Other' without condemnation. Aware of this reality, and his own narrative of non-judgemental welcome, told through the story of the prodigal son and in his encounters with the isolated and alienated, Jesus accepts the relationally pre-moral condition out of which humanity acts: 'Father, forgive them, for they do not know what they are doing' (Luke 23:34). Jesus offers this act of repentance on behalf of those who would seek to exclude the 'Other' from their lives, for he knows that reconciliation takes place when the one wronged is willing and able to absorb the cost and consequences of relational dysfunction: mistrust, self-seeking intimacy, ontological incoherence, and emotional, spiritual and physical death.

Jesus takes to the cross (the symbol of human non-being) his storied-self: an ontologically coherent self. In doing so he redeems the cross and changes its significance. There is a paradigm shift in its meaning. For by making his death on the cross the intent of his storied-self, facing this place of non-being and non-meaning and giving up his life there for 'Others', Jesus takes to it his 'at-oneness'. In doing so, it becomes *the* place, symbolically and in reality, for *the presence* of mutual, undistorted, unpolluted relating. This is the place we all must go in search of our own *at-one-ment*.

Recognizing the counter-narrative

All of this leaves the reader with one question: can the self recognize the ontological coherence, the *at-one-ment*, of Jesus in such a way as to counter one's own narrative and allow the desired liberation from a story dominated by chronic shame? In the final analysis, the answer to this question can only lie with the storied-self, for only the self can determine whether such a narrative of atonement is meaningful and sufficient to counter their plight. That said, around the cross are those who, for one reason or another, find themselves in this place of non-being and non-meaning with Jesus. These characters, who draw the focus away from Jesus, suggest that the cross is a place of meaning and sufficiency that allows the re-narration of the self. They suggest this because some go on to change their story in the light of being present at the cross.

The centurion at the foot of the cross is present because he has been charged by Rome to ensure that Jesus' crucifixion is dispatched with as little incident as possible. Although we know little about him, it is not unreasonable to suggest that he probably had no concern or personal feeling for any of the dying men who looked down on him. In this sense he would be the most relationally dispassionate of the characters who gather at Golgotha. This fact, however, makes his consciousness, his recognition of the importance of Jesus, all the more powerful. Naturally, it is not possible to insist that his statements about Jesus constitute a 'conversion' of his own personal story. However, reading this narrative has led some to state that, 'Jesus' death is the supreme moment of illumination in the story … [the meaning of which] lies implicit in the centurion's statement of recognition, in the powerful way Jesus' act of sacrificial service transforms others, including the reader of the story, to see and follow.'[155]

Although the centurion's cameo is a powerful and moving one, for the postmodern reader there are obviously more significant and meaningful interchanges between Jesus and his contemporaries. As in the acts of betrayal that illumined the reader earlier in the Passion Narratives, one such interchange is the plea of the second thief, who prefigures the centurion and the final moments of Jesus' life. Crucified next to Jesus, this second thief is deliberately narrated as taking a view of Jesus that counters that of the first. The second thief sharply rebukes the first thief for mocking Jesus, while all the time Jesus remains silent. 'The second criminal also takes responsibility for his own deeds (an aspect of repentance), admitting that his condemnation is just. He distinguishes himself from Jesus, who has been condemned unjustly.'[156] In this way the second thief is portrayed as one who recognizes Jesus' intent and wishes to be a recipient, even at this most final of hours, of the reconciliation that comes by recognition of the 'Other' crucified next to him.

By this stage in the narrative the reader has seen Judas, Peter and the first criminal all tempted to live as if God were not the author of their stories – and all have learned, perhaps the reader included, that self-justification and self-interest only lead to isolation, alienation and the inability to hold together a personal narrative. The second criminal, by contrast, is blessed with this ability: he knows the error of his (and our) ways.

Finally, and as if to emphasize the cross as a place of dehumanizing isolation, exclusion, torment and abandonment, we become aware of the utter absence of personal family or friends. All who truly knew Jesus remain at a distance – willing, perhaps, but ultimately unable to help this isolated, dying creature. Only John's Gospel softens this torment, suggesting that Jesus' mother and a disciple, possibly John himself, were close enough to be recognizable (John 19:26). Yet these tragic figures allow Jesus to interpret the meaning and significance of his death. As we have seen, Jesus takes to the cross his 'at-one-ness', making it *the* place, both symbolically and in reality, for *the presence* of mutual, undistorted, unpolluted relating. However, if the cross is to be a dying for 'Others', as he intends it to be, then those who follow him there must also live by prioritizing the 'Other', for in doing so we open our lives to that same 'at-one-ness': the presence of relational, and therefore ontological, coherence.

Therefore, as Jesus turns to look upon his mother and John, his friend, he gives each to the 'Other', to live in the presence of mutual, undistorted, unpolluted relating. Jesus had once been at the feet of John, demonstrating his intent to live for the 'Other' (John 13:1,3–5). Now we see John at the feet of Jesus being asked to love beyond himself, to *be* for the 'Other'. 'This is what Jesus thirsts for and he thirsts for it in his physical anguish, in the body which is now dried and parched, and in his spirit, which yearns that we may find unity in our uniqueness and diversity.'[157]

This narrative of atonement redirects the reader, the post-industrialized self whose relating is in one way or another *away* from the 'Other', toward the 'Other'. For it is only with the presence of the 'Other' that we can begin the journey to *at-one-ment* as a human being. When we tell the story of Jesus in a sensitive way, the post-industrialized self who lives with ontological incoherence recognizes it as a meaningful and sufficient counter-story. We learn that to live with coherence between the real- and ideal-self is to have an awareness of and to include, even submit to, the 'Other' in the stories we tell.

As we observed at the beginning of the chapter, rather paradoxically, Jesus' pursuit of death in actuality becomes the pursuit of life. The postmodern fears that, in living for the 'Other', we die to ourselves. At the cross, Jesus subverts this rationale. Living for the 'Other' (even unto death) leads us from a place of isolation, alienation and meaningless insufficiency as a human being to a coherent ontology and to a place of mutual, undistorted, unpolluted relating – to a life that conquers emotional, spiritual and (almost inexplicably) physical death. For 'the norm for humankind is not the independent person, but the emphatically related one ... In order to survive and for the self to develop, the individual must internalize or "take in" significant others.'[158]

The story of Jesus, revealed through the Passion Narrative, is an anticipatory one in that it opens up the possibility of, and enacts the potential for, our own true self to appear. It also calls on the individual to live in the world as if God were the author of his or her life – it is a call out of narrative incoherence, out of 'sin' (the absence of mutual, unpolluted, undistorted relating) and out of shame. However, this is not the entire 'story'. It must be observed that, even with Jesus' substitutionary death, the freedom to narrate the self means that *we* must be accountable for the story we tell. For to come to the story of the cross as the counter-narrative to our plight demands that we metaphorically take up the cross also.

'Sin', if we may be allowed to speak its name for a moment, is not simply that which can be spun off by centrifugal activity and so generate the perception of a 'sinless' society, but is most profoundly an issue of personhood – of ontology. Ultimately, to remove 'sin' requires the death of the self, even when a substitute victim is involved. In a painful twist of irony for the post-industrialized self, the putting to death of our relational dysfunction and chronic shame is the path to *at-one-ment*. Only when the storied-self can go through 'death' without finally dying is the hope of ontological co-herence possible.

The story of atonement does not call on readers to see Jesus as a get-out clause, one who will live a life of narrative coherence for them and allow God to author his life so that they do not have to. It is more that the reader is called to identification – an identification which, for the post-industrialized self, requires the story of the 'Other' (Judas and the other disciples) as much as the story of Jesus. For it is they who reveal the self as being without narrative (ontological) coherence. They are the ones who demonstrate what it means to live in the *absence* of mutual, unpolluted, undistorted relating. Jesus, by comparison, opens up the radical possibility of the removal of that incoherence of the self, but only by the willingness to walk a similar path of intent which will require an act of repentance: living with God as the author of our life by dying to self and embracing the 'Other' in an act of *at-one-ment*. In this way Jesus' story leads the post-industrialized self 'exactly to the "places" he must occupy with his person: on the one hand, to the place of the person rejected by God and before God; on the other hand, to the place of a child living near with God',[159] and with his, or her, fellow human beings.

IV

Indwelling the Counter-narrative: Rereading the Eucharist

10. A Rite of Identification

> Rituals and celebrations mark significant steps in the journey away from a problem story to a new and preferred vision of life.[160]

For the sake of brevity, our look at the gospel narratives ended with Jesus' final exhalation on the cross. However, beyond the cross is resurrection and the revelation gained during a journey along the road to Emmaus – a revelation hidden from the understanding of the travellers until the breaking of a handful of bread (Luke 24:30–31).

Linguistically, the claim that this event mimics the Eucharist in the Upper Room is not straightforward.[161] And why should it be? After all, the two on the road to Emmaus were not privy to the events that took place at that Passover meal. For them, it is far more likely that as Jesus 'took bread, gave thanks, broke it and gave it to them' they would recall the feeding of the multitude or, less likely, a more intimate moment of table fellowship with Jesus (Luke 24:30; cf. Luke 9:16; 22:19). However, while this is illuminating it does not account for the fact that, as readers, we too sat among the disciples on that fateful Passover night. Therefore, Emmaus' narrative proximity to the story of the Last Supper (though it did not turn out to be his 'last' supper given that, post-resurrection, Jesus continues to share in meals with others, even with us as we gather for the Eucharist) surely reminds the reader of Jesus' intent and action narrated in the Upper Room, rather than the earlier miracle. However, that the multitudes were 'satisfied' by this 'broken bread' is surely worth recalling in our search for meaning and sufficiency (Luke 9:17).

Leaving aside pedantic scholarship for the moment, it is perhaps more significant to state that such repetition of words and action allows us to suggest that not only was Jesus inclined to act ritually, but that he did so because he understood that we, too, recall, encounter and are 'converted' by such processes. So it is that the post-industrialized self is able to encounter the life-changing narrative of atonement through the eucharistic re-enactment of that night in the Upper Room; we face our own inconsistency and incoherence as we hear the liturgical words, 'Who, in the same night that he was betrayed ...'

An incarnated narrative

For the post-industrialized self, probably the most telling encounter with the accounts of Jesus' self-narration is via the church's tradition of liturgical re-enactment of that same story. In an age that Andrew Walker describes as the second orality, the communal and public act of liturgical remembrance 'is the way to the heart of the story'.[162] For not only does it provide the self with opportunity to hear, it also, through symbolic enactment, allows the whole of the sensual self to close the space/time gap and know intimately that same moment of intent, betrayal and public display of selfless sacrifice and narrative coherence. For just as the incarnation and the cross are the most significant acts of self-disclosure by a storied-being – God – so the Eucharist can be, for the storied-self, a meaningful and sufficient moment of understanding. To give it deserved epistemological status: 'Liturgy is about the *finitum copax infiniti*, the finite capacity for the infinite.'[163]

At its best, ritual is an acknowledgement that, while we are narrative beings, our stories are played out in actions as well as words. As sign-giving creatures, it is only natural that our narratives take ritual form. Indeed, we were probably sign-givers or storytellers, through acted ritual, long before we acquired the spoken and written word. Therefore, like other primitive urges, to act ritually is a felt need that is hard to resist. But more than that, by entering into the story of the Passion Narrative through the liturgy and ritual of the Eucharist, we are reminded of the reality that ideal intent must be acted out in the realm of the physical, for the body is the link between the self and the public world. Symbolic ritual, therefore, is a vital element in the re-storying of the self on its journey to *at-one-ment*.

So it is that, along with the Bible, the church's ritual of bread-breaking and wine-receiving should be seen as yet another storied event, the narrative incarnation of Jesus, that invites people to live in its world as the real world. Like film, television, novels, magazines, radio, internet, advertising and personal encounter, liturgy and ritual reach out to the postmodern with counter-narratives for the storied-self – narrative possibilities by which a new self can be told. For as in all these things, if told well, the post-industrialized self will chart the world created by the liturgical narrative in a quest for images and symbols which are meaningful and sufficient for their plight.

Ritual, however, is not a one-off event. It is, by its own literal description, repetitious. Given that re-storying and *at-one-ment* is a process, as we have already indicated at several junctures, ritual proves purposeful in these endeavours. Therefore, it must be understood that, as ritual, the Eucharist is an act of continual revelation. Like the travellers on the road to Emmaus we become aware through this ritual that Jesus journeys with us (Luke 24:15), wherever our own story has taken and will take us. It is that place where the self has revealed to his or her self – for the first time, or indeed, once more – the intent of Jesus to suffer and die for all. 'The Eucharist is the permanent centre of reference for Christ's own interpretation of his passion.'[164] It recalls the night in the Upper Room. The bread and wine signify the coming near, the being present of one thought to be absent. Therefore, whatever story we bring to the table, the Eucharist represents to us the cross – not Golgotha, that polluted place of non-being and non-meaning, but the cross of Jesus – the place, symbolically and in reality, for *the presence* of mutual, undistorted, unpolluted relating. In this way it becomes a theophany – a place of encounter between humanity and God. It is a moment when God appears to all in bread and wine and makes known, through the recital of the liturgy, his storied-self to human souls.

Many stories, many tables

Fruitful as ritual and liturgical practice can be in connecting the post-industrialized self to the counter-narrative of atonement, there is a tension and a challenge to face as the stories of our 'sinless' society encounter the traditions of the church: liturgical renewal.

If we cast our minds back to the beginning of the argument here, we recall the metaphorical use of Pentecost, to 'speak' the language of the context in which we find ourselves in order to '… tell the wonderful things God has done' (Acts 2:11, CEV). We have suggested that the Christian community has a mandate, both biblical and traditional, to contextualize the atonement by drawing on the scriptural and historical models and metaphors. However, if we are to follow this through to its logical conclusion, the rituals and liturgical practices we use to recall the atonement must also be open to renewal in order to engage meaningfully and sufficiently with the changing story of what it means to be human in the twenty-first century.

Naturally, liturgical and ritual renewal is not an easy task. To hold to tradition is for some a powerful human desire that should not be trampled on in order simply to pursue relevancy. Indeed, tradition has an important role to play in telling our story. However, the obverse of this is that our desire to preserve traditional forms of ritual and liturgical expression should not suppress or deny an urgent need to generate meaningful and sufficient practices for the 'sinless' self. Ritual and liturgy can effectively address the contemporary situation, but only if we are willing to listen to the cultural and philosophical stories being told around us, to learn the 'sign language' of the postmodern, and so engage and counter the storied-self through a renewal of our own symbolic language. 'The "language" that liturgy speaks needs to be reassessed and brought into line with the "social and cultural circumstances of time"… liturgy as a form of ritual speaks an aesthetic, symbolic language by means of action as well as word. It is not to be reduced to mere word, as if its meaning were contained totally in written text.'[165]

Though controversial on paper, in reality the history of the Christian community supports the practice of liturgical renewal. Indeed, it has even been suggested that the church in the New Testament era did not practice one standard liturgy, nor claim one single origin for the Lord's Supper, but developed and shaped its ritual to meet the specific needs of the missional context in which they found themselves.[166] This missional use of the Eucharist has been at the centre of liturgical renewal down the centuries, for it recognizes that here is a way of embodying, or incarnating, the story of atonement for future generations.

This is the lesson we must learn if we are to generate counter-stories for the post-industrialized self: liturgy is the drawing out of tradition in order to re-narrate the story of atonement for a new era. Liturgy needs to function as a form of language that is specific to context, while at the same time it needs to be the vehicle that carries the counter-narrative that brings hope and healing for the 'sinless'. In other words, the Eucharist needs to connect my story with God's story so that they become one.

> The point of the Eucharist is …to offer us a clue to what God is up to in human history. The sign-giving does not aim to take us back to the first-century; the Eucharist is not a time machine. Rather, it catches us into the stream of God's continuing and liberating activity … No symbol rooted in the order of creation could do this … [For while such] symbols speak to us of God's love [they] do not lead us into the mystery of redemption.[167]

Creating certain ambiguity

The above claims about the importance and power of ritual and liturgical practice for the storied-self perhaps need qualifying a little – not least because, in our own context, Christian ritual and liturgical practice may generate a sense of non-being for the chronically shamed self, causing rejection, inferiority, powerlessness and worthlessness. Indeed, some rituals of reconciliation and repentance, such as the practice of formal confession, can actually compound chronic shame, heighten alienation and perpetuate exclusion.[168]

These words, while sobering, are also enlightening in that they reaffirm the suspicion of others that liturgy and ritual are the encounter of one story with another. As such, the one needs to listen to the other if the encounter is to be mutually informative and healing. Or, to put it another way, the sufficiency of ritual and liturgy to counter the story of the self being brought to it depends on their ability to speak meaningfully to any given context. For that to happen, the symbolic and literal language may have to be changed, or, alternatively, there may have to be a certain ambiguity in the words and symbols used so that everyone, regardless of the stories they bring to the table, can approach and appropriate this story of *at-one-ment*.

Of course, liturgy is a vital component in shaping the identity of Christians, for it is the corporate expression of the story we come to gather around. It allows us to hear once more and internalize that story which countered our own. Through ritual action and spoken (or sung) words, Christians reaffirm who they are and their relationship with the story Jesus told in the Upper Room. It is in theory, if not always in practice and perception, an open table where we come to find acceptance, inclusion and so build our self-worth. However, there is considerable uncertainty, whether implicit or explicit, that the words and actions actually or symbolically com-municate the presence of mutual, undistorted, unpolluted relating that exists at the cross.

The importance of this is all too apparent when we listen to elements of the story the post-industrialized self tells as chronic shame consumes him or her. For in this story, the person that comes to the table perceives the self as 'being *judged to be inferior, defective, incompetent, undesirable, or unlovable.* The self has a sense that it is defective and has a basic flaw that ensures its unacceptability and rejection by those whom it loves. Shame thus contains a fear of abandonment, loss of love, and so loss of self.'[169]

Even a cursory glance at the Gospels would assure the reader that Jesus never spoke or acted in such a way that would bring these judgements to his table of fellowship. Therefore, it is only right that those who follow in this offering of table fellowship should take care to ensure that the rituals and liturgical practices that surround the Eucharist do not focus solely on the problematic story or plight of the storied-self, such as the issue of chronic shame. Indeed, the fear of exposure that this would generate would only serve to exclude, rather than include, the chronically-shamed self.

Naturally, liturgical renewal is not an easy request to make. Questions as to the extent and viability of doing this need to be addressed (though we do not have the space to properly address them here). For example, given the plight of the postmodern 'sinless' self, what function or interpretation can be given to the prayer of humble access, with its implication of non-specific sinfulness and personal unworthiness? For the chronically-shamed, to recite over and over that they are 'unworthy, even to gather the crumbs from under the table' is unlikely to be a healing mantra for the postmodern, for such acknowledgments are easily distorted by the story the self brings to the table.

Many would want to affirm that the eucharistic table is not for the worthy but for the unworthy, for this is the message of grace that pervades God's story. However, recalling our discussions about the pre-moral nature of chronic shame, we realize that this is perhaps a story that only those who already dwell in the fuller picture of the story of salvation can understand. When we line up to 'receive communion' and dwell for a moment in the story it represents we take our place, historically and narratively, behind the multitudes on the hillside, behind tax collectors and prostitutes, behind Thomas, Peter and Judas and behind those travellers on the road to Emmaus who have all eaten at the table with Jesus. Given this genealogy, rather than thinking about themselves as unworthy postmoderns are more likely to wonder: Why are prostitutes and sinners, Judas 'the betrayer' and Peter, the one who denied Jesus, all eating at the table, while we are not even allowed to concern ourselves with mopping up the crumbs that fall our way?

What all this tells us is that how a person 'feels' when they come to the table needs to be taken extremely seriously. Too often, liturgy and ritual serve to flatten out the emotional experience of the self, denying the natural, almost intuitive relationship between our feelings and their public expression through action. Ritual, therefore, should prioritize the outlet of emotion. We should be developing ritual and liturgy that encourage the storied-self to speak in words and action and so connect their story with the elements of the meal, carrying the postmodern self into the narrative of atonement in the way it represents itself to them.

Ultimately, the point of representing the intent and actions of Jesus in the Eucharist is that through this ritual the divine story shapes our story and is able to take on new intuitive and creative dimensions through the creature who images God. As such, even with a story surrounding them, the elements are not truth-stating objects but symbols – at one and the same time ambiguous and yet pregnant with meaning. This is their beauty (and is the beauty of all ritual): the signs of the atonement are multilingual.

Not only does ritual connect with our most basic, most primitive self, but through its ambiguity it allows us to reflect God's image as imaginative, creative, self-storying creatures. Therefore, we can make the signs of *at-one-ment* meaningful for our own plight. As we take and eat, placing the bread upon our tongue, we are able to 'place' this symbol and action into our own story, making it meaningful and sufficient, allowing us to identify with and appropriate the counter-narrative of atonement that it represents to us.

Our ritual and liturgical practice needs to acknowledge that the post-industrialized self is used to reading and generating meaning from signs and symbols. They are used to this intuitively because they are human beings and culturally because of the sign-giving context in which they live. Therefore, they can make meaningful and sufficient the symbols of bread and wine, interpreting them for their own specific plight while allowing the eucharistic narrative to remain a story that sheds light on our understanding of 'sin' as an issue of relational and narrative incoherence. The bread's brokenness comes, then, to represent the cross and the absence of mutual, undistorted, unpolluted relating that brings about the need for atonement. In eating the bread, the post-industrialized self is asked to recall that *at-one-ment* requires brokenness to be absorbed.

The death and resurrection of the storied-self

The Eucharist is that rite of identification that allows for the atoning work of Jesus to manifest itself in the lives of those who encounter the narrative. It is that moment when, narratively speaking, the 'death' of the self can occur and the possibility of divine authorship can become a real possibility. In this way, the Eucharist has its most profound and poignant effect in putting to death the narrative incoherence of the storied-self while at the same time bringing forth life after death in the form of a new, narratively coherent self.

The recipients of this life-that-denies-death must be careful, however, not to forget where their hope lies. For the symbolic acts of eating and drinking are without meaning if they become rites set adrift from the moorings of their prior narrative – the story of atonement. Just as the cross was nothing without the intent and selfless actions of Jesus, so, too, the Eucharist is nothing without those narratives in which Jesus reveals his intent and subsequent actions that prove his coherent ontology. It is precisely those narratives, combined with the symbolic act, which make the eucharistic meal a rite of identification. What is more, in that identification the recipient is drawn into the story in such a way that Jesus' intent now becomes the desire of the self. Sykes recognizes this partnership: 'The ritual eating and drinking of the Eucharistic elements and the performance of the narratives are together indicative of an interior intention; and it is by means of both (the rituals and the intention) that the proclamation of the meaning of Christ's death is constantly remade in the world.'[170] As the Eucharist proceeds and the narrative of Jesus' intent, betrayal, forgiveness and eventual self-oblation is realized, the rite of identification calls on those present to offer and reorientate their lives in a similar way.

11. A Confrontation with Self

> The consciousness of the failure of the self . . . is a necessary phase in the process whereby human beings are liberated to become themselves.[171]

The liturgy that surrounds the Eucharist places words into our mouths and gives us actions for our bodies that enable us to enter into the story of atonement we encounter in this ritual. These words and actions are not such that they come to dominate the storied-self, or take us to a place we do not wish to go. However, as we dwell momentarily in this counter-narrative, we are not always allowed to be comfortable. For while the Eucharist is ultimately that place where we come to see, hear and 'taste' the Christian story of *at-one-ment*, it is far more than simply a retelling of the intent of Jesus. By ritual action and liturgical text we are confronted with our own storied-self, with our inadequacies and chronic shame, with the absence of mutual, undistorted, unpolluted relating. However, we are not left in this place of narrative incoherence but are called to move beyond the inadequacies of the storied-self, into a new story of *at-one-ment*.

A pre-moral confession

We spoke above of the desire for liturgical renewal and the need for ambiguity in the signs and words that become our rituals so that, whatever story is brought to the table, the narrative of *at-one-ment* told by the Eucharist can be approached and appropriated by all. Indeed, we even went as far as to suggest that ultimately what may be needed are new and additional signs and symbols that are more meaningful and sufficient for the post-industrialized self. In being an open table, alongside community and traditional liturgical expression, the Eucharist needs to leave space for sign-making, the genesis of which must be the story 'What it means to be a person living in a post-industrialized, post-Christian society'. However, as we have also said, for some liturgical renewal is not an easy or necessarily welcome task. It is therefore essential, if we are to affirm and continue with our current liturgical practices, to consider how the 'sinless' might respond to a tradition that requires the repetition of the words:

> We have sinned against you and against our neighbour,
> in what we have said and done,
> through ignorance, through weakness, through our own
> deliberate fault.

These words hold little meaning for the postmodern storied-self. Primarily they are not 'sinners' in the story they tell – except possibly in their failure at 'project self'. But where is the 'sin' against the self in our liturgical practice? For while *at-one-ment* is very much about reconciliation to the 'Other', it is also about the self. The *absence* of mutual, undistorted, unpolluted relating is a 'sin' against one's own humanness, a denial of the coherent ontology by which we image the God who created us.

Secondly, while we have emphasized that personal *at-one-ment* requires the self to prioritize the 'Other' in the story we tell, confronting postmoderns with the accusation that they have wronged a neighbour is unlikely to bring a reconciling consideration of the 'Other'. Thirdly, and perhaps most alien of all, is the concept of fault. The post-industrialized self is *sinned against*, not sinner. They are the helpless victims of social structures, institutions and corporate bodies. It is with these perpetrators that responsibility lies, not with the 'innocent victims' of their distorted practices. Obligations and responsibilities lie fairly and squarely with institutions in the story the post-industrialized self tells. Therefore, there are no duties they have failed to fulfil, no forbidden acts about which they should feel guilty, no 'sins' that need confessing.

All this negativity does not, however, mean that our liturgical practices, as they stand, are utterly meaningless and insufficient in confronting the storied-self with a narrative of atonement for their own plight. For while the post-industrialized self may not read liturgy in the way we would wish, even in this particular story of 'sin' there is a counter-narrative for the postmodern 'sinless' self.

These confessional words can point the hearer, as did the narratives that spoke of the disciples' desertion of Jesus, to the fact that our failings, our relational inadequacies and the resulting 'betrayal' of 'Others' and ourselves, are not deliberate acts per se. Though on occasion the storied-self (*what we have said and done*) may be sufficiently aware of the grammar of relating to consciously act in a way that damages relationship with 'Others' *through our own deliberate fault*, more often than not the storied-self is generated out of *ignorance and weakness.* To recall Jesus' own words once more, *they do not know what they are doing* for they are, socially and relationally, *pre-moral.* Their failing is an ontological one, beyond the ability of the self to act differently, living as they do in the absence of mutual, undistorted, un-polluted relating.

The story of the 'sinless' postmodern self should not be decried. Rather, it should be accepted as a valid narrative to bring to the Eucharist. This is, after all, still a plight that requires *at-one-ment.* Indeed, it needs it as much as, if not more than, a story of sin as moral misdemeanour, for this is a plight of relational absence. The words *'against you and against our neighbour'* may prove to be anathema to some who gather at the table. In the context of the entire ritual, however, these words can bring the post-modern 'sinless' self to an awareness of the absence of 'Others', to the *absence* of mutual, undistorted, un-polluted relating and, eventually, even to the absence of God. Once an individual is within the narrative recited and recalled during the Eucharist, this process of 'conscientization' begins. Therefore, given time and the right emphasis, ritual and liturgy can confront the post-modern self and effectively 'positivize' chronic shame and the ontological and relational incoherence that follows it, turning them into points of departure towards a counter-story of ontological coherence and *at-one-ment.*

An 'Old' example of the counter-narrative

At this stage, with the post-industrialized self being confronted with a possible counter-narrative for their plight, we turn from the intensity of the atonement narrative to consider another story which serves to bring clarity to the role narrative plays in raising awareness of our relational dysfunction.

In 2 Samuel, David, King of Israel, has done much to 'betray' his relationship with 'Others'.[172] More crucially, he has come to a point of self-justification, denying the dysfunction his betrayals have wrought not only in his relationships with others, but more importantly in his relationship with God. He has become the centre of his world. He has begun to tell his story, to self-narrate his existence, in isolation from the narratives of 'Others' and of God. Though he would not express it in this way, he is generating a 'sinless' self through self-centred justification.

Into this storied world comes a counter-story as the prophet Nathan retells the events. Only by this alternative story, this narrative possibility, is David's conscience pricked. Nathan brings David a meaningful and sufficient story through which *at-one-ment* is made possible.

A similar process is happening in the encounter between the post-industrialized self and the narratives of the Christian community, in particular as the gospel narratives are retold at the Eucharist. When the Christian community recites the betrayal of Judas, the failing of the disciples and the ontological and narrative coherence of Jesus and links such narratives with our own through liturgical practice and ritual, it does for the postmodern storied-self exactly what Nathan did for David. As individuals living in a 'sinless' society we learn of our need for atonement 'not by beginning with allegedly universal observations about the "human condition" but, rather, by beginning with a story of redemption'.[173] Through this counter-narrative, the post-industrialized self is revealed as one who lives in relational dysfunction, in the absence of the 'Other'. As such, we become self-centred and self-justifying. By doing as David did, by allowing the self to become the centre of the world, by the hubris of becoming author and finisher of our narrative, we deny God his rightful place in our lives. As Gestrich argues, 'We all take the place of God when we make the world into a world centred around us.'[174]

This is the 'sin' that pervades our 'sinless' society: 'our determined effort to live our lives as if God were not the author of our lives'.[175] The result is an inevitable dysfunction in all of our relationships. Atonement, there-fore, must be found in the counter-narrative that begins with Adam's desire to narrate his own life; continues with the history of God's people, Israel, who sought often to do the same; and finally encounters the betrayal and failings of the disciples that call our own to mind. The apex of this narrative is discovered in the intent, testing, submission and narrative coherence of Jesus. This is the story we recall and live out in the liturgy of the Eucharist. The Eucharist is a place for the post-industrialized self, isolated by chronic shame, to discover, perhaps for the first time, the presence of the 'Other', to be made at-one, to be reconciled and authored once more by the Creator who made us storied-beings.

For some, such rereadings are helpful. Others feel that they do violence to the text, being *eisegesis* (reading into a text the meaning one wants to get out of it) of the worst kind. Even so, in returning to the context of the post-industrialized self confronted with the story of atonement in the liturgical practices of the Christian community, the issue of meaning and sufficiency still has to be addressed.

It may well be that many find a narrative disparate to their own storied-self serves them well in countering their personal story and they are willing and able to enter into, be 'converted' by, and so re-story their self through adopting it as their own. However, as postmodernity deepens, our societies become increasingly post-Christian. In this 'sinless' society, where chronic shame stalks the self and relating is so often a selfish endeavour, it will be difficult for a narrative that is far removed from the story of the self and its plight and aspirations to become a narrative possibility, however good the promise of its 'final chapter'. This is why the Christian community needs to reassess its narrative of atonement – biblically, historically and in light of the contemporary stories it encounters. We need to ask hard questions about the appropriateness of our liturgical and ritual practice for communicating meaningfully and sufficiently this same narrative of atonement for a 'sinless' society. And perhaps, at the very least, we need to create an open, non-judgemental table of fellowship that can be approached without fear of exposure or exclusion. This table should be, like the cross it represents, a place for the *presence* of mutual, undistorted, unpolluted relating, a symbol of *at-one-ment* in a relationally fractured world.

A brief liturgy for a 'sinless' society

The post-industrialized self can potentially come into contact with many 'Nathans'. As we have noted, counter-stories come to the postmodern through all kinds of media: film, television, novels, magazines, radio, internet, advertising and personal encounter. So, too, therapists and psychoanalysts can be 'Nathans' for the storied-self searching for meaning and sufficiency in a post-Christian, 'sinless' society. Therefore, it is paramount that the Christian community think of their ritual and liturgical practice as fulfilling the role of Nathan: bringing to the post-industrialized storied-self a counter-narrative that can be approached, tried and appropriated as meaningful and sufficient for their plight. However, it must be a liturgy that is recognizable to the post-industrialized self as one that carries something of their own story – or, at the very least, it must leave space so that their story can be told. Liturgy and ritual should serve two purposes: they should allow the storied-self to encounter a narrative possibility, a counter-story, that is meaningful and sufficient for his or her plight; but liturgy and ritual should also allow the self to be con-fronted with the personal story that he or she brings to this encounter.

With this in mind, what follows is a brief liturgy for the 'sinless' self. I am not a liturgist and so offer this with some reservation. It is a personal 'play' with ideas rather than a suggestion as to the direction liturgy should go, if indeed it should be renewed at all. That said, others may be able to develop these words into something meaning-ful and sufficient for those who bring a 'sinless' story to the eucharistic table.

A Table of Fellowship

On the night that he was 'betrayed',
Jesus ate with his friends: 'betrayers' and self-betrayed, one and all.

Jesus broke bread and gave it to his friends
As a sign of his intent to die that they might have life.

He also shared wine with them
A symbol of his death
That opened to humankind the possibility of reconciliation to God,
To ourselves and to Others.

So we also come to the table of Jesus,
For that is what he desires.

We come to reflect on his story.
But we also come to reflect on our own story
And on the stories of those we love and those we struggle to love.

We acknowledge the absence of the Other in our lives – both human and divine.
We have told our story for far too long
Isolated from the Other.

As we acknowledge the inadequacies of our own story, we say that we are sorry.
For out of ignorance and weakness,
We have not found space in our stories for the presence of God
We have not found space in our stories for the presence of Others.

Though we are not against You
We have failed at being for You.
You have been absent from our lives.
As a result, we are against ourselves, for we are Your Creation.

Therefore, we lift our heads to gaze upon the cross and listen to these words of hope:
"Forgive them, for they do not know what they are doing."

Like prodigal child, we bring our story to the table of Jesus
Assured by the story of the Lord's Supper that we will find fellowship there.

We come
Without fear of exposure
Without fear of judgement
For this is the Lord's Table.

Though we withdraw from You
And from Others

You do not withdraw from us
And so we thank You.

Our presence at this table means that we are Your friends.

So, as we approach this table of fellowship
We recall those absent from our lives
And acknowledge the presence of Others here with us.

We gather
That we may become one with ourselves
One with each Other
One with God.

Though we fear it.
We also come to this table so that we,
Like You,
Can 'die' to ourselves.
This is our Golgotha
This is our cross.
For we know and understand that in dying
We open ourselves up to the presence
Of Others in our lives.

Therefore, we offer Others a sign of peace
A symbol of our desire for the Other to be part of our story
And for ourselves to be part of the Other.

We come in the hope of *at-one-ment*.
That we may be reconciled to Others
And to the Other: God.

At this table,
In this moment,
We are given another chance.
To put aside our denial of the Other
And embrace the story of Jesus as our own story.

God, into Your hands we place our lives.
We look to Your story to become part of our story
And so be *at-one* with You, with Others and with ourselves.

Amen.

12. An Act of 'Communion'

I receive life from all around me: To all around me I give
life.[176]

We need, finally, to draw attention to one other important
dimension of the Eucharist: Where does the story take
place? For the post-industrialized self, wrestling with
issues of chronic shame and the *absence* of mutual, undistorted, unpolluted relating, the fact that the Eucharist
is a communal activity and not simply a rite of identification, or a confrontation with self acted out in isolation, is
vital. The 'sinless' self, after all, has a desperate need and
desire for 'communion'.

What brings significance to the Eucharist is the fact
that, after the narratives of atonement are reworked into
the ritual and liturgical practice of the community, the re-
enactment of those narratives takes place in the presence
of 'Others' within that community. For it is here, with the
'Other' and before the 'Other', that the 'testing' of the
individual's intent first takes place. Just as Jesus faced the
challenge of Gethsemane and the fear of failing in his
resolve to go to the cross, now also the individual, who
must face his or her own dying to self, is called to deny

self-seeking and self-justification and embrace the 'Other' in an act of mutual forgiveness and *at-one-ment*. The individual's real-self is illuminated by such encounter. 'Revelation becomes an experienced reality at the juncture where the narrative identity of an individual collides with the narrative identity of the Christian community.'[177] The individual's narrative identity is characterized by relational *absence*, ontological in-coherence, distrust of the self, the inability to be faithful to the ideal-self, and also by the fear of failing, which leads to the intimate and emotional exclusion of the 'Other'. By comparison, the identity of the community (if indeed it lives out the narrative of atonement it gathers round) is one of inclusion, where the self is called to 'confess' their old self and embrace or 'convert' to a new narrative, so that they may be *at-one* with their self and the 'Other', allowing reconciliation to occur.

Confessions from the edge to the centre

Of course, this 'call to confess' by the Christian community creates an impasse for the self, who is suffering under the isolating narrative of post-industrial shame, to confess. We have already observed that, for an individual faced with guilt, confession could be seen as a cathartic experience. But since the primary victim of shame is the self, the speaking out of that shame in an intentional manner, such as a confession, is unlikely to occur. Being asked to narrate oneself in a form that may be seen as a confession, particularly one-to-one in, for example, a therapist/client or priest/parishioner relationship, is only likely to bring silence – or, worse, a false cover story to throw the 'Other' off the scent. This is a situation to be pitied, for without confession there can be no atonement and therefore none of the intimacy that the self craves, which can only come through reconciliation with the 'Other' that generates mutual, undistorted, unpolluted relating.

In the act of the Eucharist, however, there is perhaps the hope of moving beyond such an impasse. For within ritual and liturgical practice there is space not only to hear the story being told, but also for the individual to consider and to tell his or her own story – even to confess. But the self will not confess to one whose narrative he or she does not trust. Nor is this a confession in isolation, as if the self and his or her narrative identity is the centre of attention. This is a confession made not in embarrassing autonomy, but in supportive community. It is a confession made in the light of the hope that comes from Jesus' narrative of self-coherence achieved through the maintaining of relationships with 'Others', even with that of his betrayer.

The Eucharist should be an open table – not theoretically, but in reality. As such, the chronically shamed, narratively incoherent, 'sinless' self should feel comfortable to be on the edge of the encounter, never pressured to take part, to speak or act in a way that is not bearable for them at any given moment. At the same time, however, the 'sinless' self should feel welcome to 'approach' as and when they are ready to do so – to receive the sustenance of grace that pervades the bread and wine; to have their story countered by the eucharistic narrative of atonement; to re-narrate their story in light of it; to be moved almost imperceptibly into the presence of mutual, undistorted, unpolluted relating. Rather perceptively, the individual's relationship to the Christian community and the Eucharist has been thought of thus: 'First table fellowship, then repentance and membership of the new community. This seems … a far more beautiful and gracious practice than setting preconditions on coming to "the Lord's table" – something the Lord never did.'[178]

At its most basic and yet useful level, the liturgy that surrounds the eucharistic ritual gives words to the silenced-self, struck dumb by the fear of exposure. It is, for the post-industrialized storied-self, a 'myth', a possible story into which they enter and momentarily become a part. Rather like an actor in a play, the chronically shamed self can for a time play a role, become part of another story or simply watch from the wings, observing the 'play' unfold, considering if this is a story that can ever be meaningful and sufficient for their plight. However, if *at-one-ment* is ever to occur, then the individual must be brought to a place of confession if they are truly going to understand their self and enter into a human identity as a storied-being in the image of God, for it is here that the self is opened up to alternative narration.

To tell their story through this narrative of atonement is in itself an act of confession. Indeed, it is an act of repentance, in the sense that to begin to tell their story in this way is the self saying that they have found a better way to be. Like Judas, the incoherent storied-self is put to death. Unlike Judas, this self dies in exchange for a new story – a meaningful and sufficient counter-narrative. The storied-self is 'resurrected' through the retelling of the self in line with the eucharistic story of atonement, mirroring the death and resurrection of Jesus and in anticipation of a physical reality yet to come. For it is the leaving behind of the self, whose plot line was one of relational absence, for a story of *at-one-ment* as told by Jesus.

Traumatic as this may be for the postmodern self, confessing with words is the easy part. For, taken as a whole, the Eucharist is the retelling of Jesus' intent – an intent publicly acted out in his physical body. To speak of the 'Other' in our stories is one thing, to reach out and embrace the 'Other', physically and emotionally, is an entirely different human endeavour. As our 'brief liturgy for a "sinless" society' suggested, we need to accept that we have dysfunction and, in learning to do this, we need to be open to embracing the 'Other'. In this way, it is possible to speak of the idea of confession as 'a relational form of understanding, for self-understanding in Christian narrative always involves a relation between the self and a significant other – that community which recites and lives the narrative and finally and ultimately, that reality called "God" who is the narrative's true subject'.[179]

The encounter between self and community can be a healing one. It allows 'long-silenced voices to tell for themselves stories that question and counter those that dominate and oppress'.[180] It also flags up the responsibility of the community to live and act in such a way that 'thickens' rather than denies the new story of the 'sinless' or chronically shamed person that is beginning to emerge from the narrative of atonement. For as we begin to 'confess' and 'repent' by re-storying ourselves, the community becomes a witness to the emerging self. There is a ready-made 'audience' that not only verifies the existence of the new narrative but that also, significantly, adds life and richness to the storied-self by linking their own stories to it. To make the 'Other' significant in this way is important, for, at its birth, our new storied-self has the 'Other' written into the centre of the plot.

Finally, and importantly, it must be understood that the 'Other' does not have be a physical reality at the eucharistic table. Indeed, psychologically, community can consist of people present or absent from the table, real or imaginary, from the person's past or present.

Significant 'characters' from other stories form part of the community in which the storied-self lives. This allows the Christ of the Eucharist or, indeed, God himself, to become a vital member of the 'audience' in thickening the story of the post-industrialized self. Indeed, it is vital that the postmodern self hears the version of his or her story told by God, for the narrative of atonement originates from the imagination and the love of this storied-being, in whose image we are made.

The Eucharist as mutual presence

At the heart of the Eucharist is a declaration of commonality: *though we are many, we are one, because we all share in the one loaf*. Naturally, the *'one loaf'* is a sign that reminds us of the Upper Room, of the Passover meal shared between Jesus and his friends. It should also, however, remind us of the narrating of Jesus' intent and the fact that, like us, Jesus was a person who made sense of his self and the world around him through narration. In short, he was and is a storied-self. Given that this is so, the *one loaf* motif should also be understood as a declaration that we all share in the *one story* – the story of atonement retold and re-enacted at the Eucharist.

That said, we must be careful. For to speak of the 'one' story is not a statement that requires narrative uniformity from those who gather around the Lord's table. If we recall the Last Supper, as we are invited to do during the Eucharist, then we should be acutely aware that alongside Jesus' own story there are other stories being told. Indeed, Jesus invites them to be told, for his table is never a place where one person's story is called upon to dominate others – even Jesus' own. That is, while we are called to make Jesus' story of atonement our own, we are encouraged to remain unique acts of creation in that we all continue to tell a personal story – a sub-plot within the story of atonement. Therefore, if we return to the eucharistic announcement that *'we are one'*, we see that it is because *we share in the one loaf* (or story) and not that *we share in the one loaf* because we are simply the same in some generic sense. Indeed, *we are many* and are allowed to stay that way because 'sameness' is a dimension of the kind of 'thin' stories that only perpetuate our plight.

The eucharistic table is one of fellowship precisely because it welcomes a diversity of stories – even the 'sinless' story of the postmodern. Alongside this story, however, comes the narrative possibility, the counter-story of atonement that informs and so 'thickens' the story of the self. The narrative of atonement counters and redeems our own. But the story we are left with is still our own, and not someone else's. We remain within the uniqueness in which we were created rather than being brought under a self-destroying metanarrative. For while we are called to put to death the incoherent story by which we live, there is a 'resurrection' in that we are given a new, coherent story. For this is the paradox and the beauty of 'resurrection' – it is an event that is in continuity as well as discontinuity with what preceded it.

To return to an earlier topic, the quest for a universal truth, *the story*, which typically identifies much of our religious and theological thought and practice, has a tendency to deny diversity in storytelling. As such, it encourages 'Sameness' over the 'Otherness'. This is slightly ironic, given the fact that Christianity thinks it privileges the 'Other' when in fact it privileges 'Sameness'. The result of this has been that the 'Other', when understood as the storied-self, has been given little credence or status in atonement narratives. Indeed, the 'Other' has been dominated by the 'thin' story of sin as moral misdemeanour, which has been placed on them from outside their own story, leading to meaninglessness and insufficiency when encountering narratives of atonement.

Alongside this, the drive to 'Sameness' causes a division between 'Us' and 'Them'. As such, rituals and liturgical practices, like the Eucharist, which are supposed to deny the absence of relational dysfunction and instead promote the *presence*, if only symbolically at times, of mutual, undistorted, unpolluted relating, have been used to demarcate an in-group and an out-group – 'sinners'. Add that to the autonomous philosophies of the Enlightenment and the Eucharist becomes, as it so often has, an individual at a table faced with an awesome sacrifice for sin instead of a table of fellowship where a community gathers to retell a story of *at-one-ment*.

In order to allow the presence of the 'Other' in our story (in any story), we need to accept the 'Other' story as authentic and valid – even if it does not appear to fit readily into our understanding of the self in relation to God or our narratives of atonement. We need to be open to the possibility that the story of the 'sinless' self is valid, even if we don't immediately recognize it as sin, or as something that the cross deals with. To privilege the post-industrialized storied-self requires the understanding that 'sin', as the absence of mutual, undistorted, un-polluted relating, is a communal activity. Therefore, as a community we work with God to restore our relationships with each 'Other' and with God. A story of *at-one-ment* requires a communal response. The 'sinner' and the 'sinned against' are inseparable. There is no 'Us' and 'Them', for there is a mutuality around the table: *Though we are many, we are one, for we all share in the one loaf* (story of atonement). As Stephen Pattison rightly acknowledges, 'Rituals such as eating or worshipping, whether formal or informal, often have the effect of binding individuals and groups closer together. In creating a sense of group solidarity and well-being, they help people to de-objectify themselves and to forget their sense of shame.'[181]

We need to privilege the 'Other' in the story we tell around the table of fellowship, for in doing so we privilege the self – because the orientation of our story is such that we desire to tell a story in which the presence of mutual, undistorted, unpolluted relating is key to the plot. 'Having been embraced by God, we must make space for others in ourselves and invite them in',[182] for this is what it means to be human, this is what it means to have a coherent ontology – to be at-one.

However, without the transference of this story of *at-one-ment* into our 'no-liturgical', ordinary lives, the Eucharist, indeed Jesus' intent, has failed in its purpose. For the liturgical practice of embracing the 'Other' needs to reach beyond the boundary of mere ritual and become a defining part of the story, *'What it means to be a person living in a post-industrialized, post-Christian society'.* However, this may be a long process for the chronically shamed, storied-self living in a 'sinless' society. Until then, they must be allowed many opportunities to come and see that 'the Eucharist is the ritual time in which we celebrate [the] divine "making-space-for-us-and-inviting-us-in"'.[183] It is that moment when we understand the story of the prodigal son, the place where we encounter the welcoming father who accepts us as we are – isolated, alienated and fragmented – and so creates a valued self out of a chronically shamed, self-despising individual, absorbing the pain and trauma generated out of the absence of mutual, undistorted, unpolluted relating. It is also the place where all 'stones' of judgement and wrath are laid to rest. It is a shame-destroying, person-affirming inclusive 'telling-place' where our 'sinless' *pre-moral* story of relating is listened to without condemnation. It is a table of fellowship, where 'betrayer' and 'betrayed' eat together from the one loaf. But it is also that place of narrative possibility, where we hear, perhaps for the first time, the intent of Jesus to make *at-one-ment* from relational disunity, to make possible the *presence* of mutual, undistorted, unpolluted relating. It is the narrative moment in which we are called to go with Jesus to Golgotha, the place of human non-being, to put to death our ontologically incoherent, storied-self and exchange it for a meaningful and sufficient counter-story – a story of *at-one-ment* for a 'sinless' society.

The End of the Beginning:
Some Closing Thoughts

Many have tried to tell the story of what God has done among us ... (Luke 1:1, CEV)

If all that has gone before is thought of as a narrative mirror, then we must accept that not everyone who gazes into it will recognize themselves. Indeed, if they could, then the premise on which much of this argument is built would be wrong. For there would indeed be a story of salvation, with one plot line, a metanarrative or a single counter-story, perhaps even a 'thin' description that would suffice for all peoples everywhere in bringing about a meaningful and sufficient engagement with the Christian community's narrative of atonement. However, I remain convinced that the biodiversity that God creates in the domain of nature extends into the narration of personal history. Uniqueness is a universal narrative theme, which denies the possibility of all peoples at all times speaking with the same voice. Therefore, the concept of post-industrialized shame or a story of being 'sinless' will not be in the telling of all who come to the narrative or the table of the carpenter from Nazareth. Indeed, many will know their sin and be assured of their guilt. But if the story of Jesus narrates a 'once and for all' act of atonement, then in its telling and retelling must be a story that encounters and counters the personal narrative of all who come to see and hear, however they make account for themselves.

Whether consciously or subconsciously, all have 'sinned' and fallen short of the glory of God. A glory revealed in the mutuality of the Trinity and in God's relationship to his creation, but a glory tainted by the *absence* of mutual, undistorted, unpolluted relating with each Other. 'Sin', even for those assured of their guilt, is often explicitly, and always implicitly, a relational issue. Jesus, therefore, ever remains a figure of self-consistency in his relating, even for those unaccustomed to the idea of post-industrialized chronic shame. He ever remains a model for imitation, a sacrifice who identifies with us and a substitute who leads us to the place we all must occupy. In this sense, 'Jesus' story is but the start of a story, which both retells his story and extends it in an indeterminate fashion, producing ever new, non-identical repetitions.'[184]

These non-identical repetitions, which make up the cacophony of human telling, take place in the ever-lengthening shadow of the resurrection. Whatever else belongs in our personal history, we are more than postmodern, more than post-industrial, more than post-Christian. These transient concepts must ultimately allow room for the reality that we are, forever, post-resurrection. As Colin Gunton states, 'We are finite beings, on the way to salvation, moving between the resurrection of Jesus and the completion of our pilgrimages.'[185] Therefore, though we have barely touched upon the resurrection, suggesting only in the briefest of terms the role its real and symbolic presence plays in the narrative of atonement, it should be clear that it serves to reinforce and affirm the self-consistency of Jesus. For here is recognition that the *absence* of mutual, undistorted, unpolluted relating, which leads ultimately to death, is anathema within Jesus' ontology – so much so that death has no hold on him. The resurrection is not an addendum or a postscript. What is true of Jesus and his atoning work up to and including his final moments on the cross is also true, indeed more so, once the tomb is empty. 'The resurrection does not go back on what has gone before; it comes after and moves on.'[186] What is promised by the resurrection has its origins firmly rooted in the narrative accounts that lead from the Upper Room to Golgotha.

What is also true is that this Jesus remains distinct even when he submits his self-narration, his personal history, to the authorship of God. Jesus, in his desire to live for 'Others' and allow authorship to transcend himself, is not absorbed into that 'Other'. His resurrection is affirmation of his self because it is here that his true identity is revealed. So it is that we also, as our narration is countered by the narrative identity of this same Jesus at the Eucharist and as we acknowledge the 'Other' and allow the authorship of God, are turned outwards to the world as 'ourselves'. We are, as Thiselton would have it, 'a reconstituted selfhood of the same identity'.[187] In this sense, resurrection is nothing more than the completion of the divine purpose to keep us in our humanity, but it does so in such a way as to liberate us into an ontology of true personhood. 'What is redeemed is not just the soul, but the whole person, and since personal history is what gives a person his or her identity, it is personal history that is redeemed and preserved within the life of God.'[188] A life resurrected.

Also conspicuous by its absence is any talk of the Spirit in the process of atonement and 'conversion'. Partly, this is because of the restriction of space, coupled with the text's own silence as to precisely the role that the Spirit plays in the narrative. For the Holy Spirit is indeed both important and significant. It is, perhaps, only with theological reflection and later New Testament writings that it may be seen that this Jesus is ultimately enabled in his relatedness to the 'Other', and in his own narrative coherence, by the relationship he already has with the Spirit. Or, to simplify: Jesus' ontological coherence comes ultimately not from his 'godness' as the Second Person of the Divine Trinity, but because of his relationship to the Third Person – the Spirit of God. By implication, this must also be true of all who seek a similar liberating narrative. We are freed from our self-seeking and self-justifying and enabled to love and be loved only by the presence of the Spirit in our lives – a Spirit who becomes part of our personal history as we 'confess', allowing God to become the author of our lives.

This is not to say that we are delivered from the 'sins' against our neighbours. Our lives still testify against us. We do not live with the same ontological coherence of Jesus. The *absence* of mutual, undistorted, unpolluted relating is still at times our 'sin'. However, along with the resurrection, the Spirit gives us an eschatological hope of truly being related to each other and to God. 'The directedness of our life is now determined by the pull of the Spirit to completion rather than the pull of sin to dissolution.'[189] The Spirit opens the self to the counter-story and grafts us ever deeper into the plot.

Finally, it must be seen that the fears and the lack of trust present among the inhabitants of a post-industrialized society are vanquished: through the narrative and ontological coherence of Jesus; through the Spirit who enables us to love and be loved; and through the confessing that allows the authoring of our lives by

God. No longer are we afraid to 'merge' with the 'Other', crippled by our lack of trust in ourselves. We are now open to the 'Other' because we are open to the radical possibility that we can trust our own personal narrative. Through Jesus' own self-giving, we are assured that 'a love in which a self genuinely gives itself to the other in the interests of the other dissolves the acids of suspicion and deception'.[190] We no longer have to play the role of the victim to be empowered, for our identity is no longer in our own narration but in the words of the 'Other', our Creator. And in that narration we are declared free from the post-industrialized shame that has haunted us, free from the fear of failing our ideal-self. We are, like Jesus, people of narrative coherence. We are finally liberated to seek reconciliation because we are reconciled to ourselves. As Brümmer wisely puts it, 'If I know that God accepts me, it would be meaningless for me not to accept myself'.[191] And if I can accept myself, then the barriers that prevented me from accepting the 'Other' and seeking the intimacy I so desperately crave are, once and for all, removed.

Let the Conversation Begin:
A Response to Alan Mann

Robin Parry

Author of *Worshipping Trinity: Coming Back to
the Heart of Worship*

I'd like to thank Alan for this exceptionally thought-provoking and original contribution to Christian mission and theology. My words here are offered as a celebration of his reflections as well as a respectful call for some clarification and modification. I offer any criticisms in a spirit of Christian respect and love.

Alan is correct in claiming that the concept of sin as 'an offence against God' is increasingly abandoned. Not, I suspect, because people cannot understand what it means but rather because God is not perceived as relevant to their day to day lives. It is only to be expected that a post-God culture will become a post-sin culture but this shift does present serious missional challenges. The gospel story of God's answer to the problem of sin is heard by many postmoderns as *irrelevant* even if not as incomprehensible. Basically, it does not scratch where they itch. Alan is to be commended for taking the bull by the horns and facing the challenges head-on. I accept, like Alan, Karl Barth's comment that 'Dogmatics as such does not ask what the apostles and prophets said but what *we* must say on the basis of the apostles and prophets' (Barth, *Church Dogmatics* 1/2, 868, italics mine). Biblical faith, to remain authentic, must constantly re-imagine itself and this is the task in which Alan is rightly engaged.

I appreciate the fact that Alan offers his account not as *the* account of atonement for all people, everywhere, nor as a *replacement* for alternative more traditional accounts (although he does question the relevance of such accounts *in our context*). Rather it is offered as *an* account of atonement which will enable *some* postmodern people to be reconciled to God, others and themselves.

Alan's call for 'thick descriptions' of the human plight and of God's atonement is crucial and needs to be heard. His call for our diagnoses of the human plight to listen carefully to the concrete voices of *real* people and how *they perceive* their plight is perhaps even prophetic. Whilst I have problems with some of his claims (see later) I do want to hear his call. It is indeed the case that Christians often tend towards reductionist accounts of sin which fail to appreciate the depth and breadth of it. This, in turn, usually leads to reductionist accounts of atonement. Alan is quite right to protest against the 'thin' pre-packed theology which reduces the salvation story to sin – wrath – penal substitution – forgiveness. However, this is not to say that we must abandon talk of 'sin', 'wrath', 'penal substitution' and 'forgiveness' for postmoderns, merely that we must supplement, broaden and deepen it.

Alan seeks to supplement traditional theology with an alternative understanding of sin as 'shame' rather than of sin as 'violation of divine, moral injunctions'. 'Shame', as Alan uses the word, refers to the *self*-judgement with which a person indicts themself because of the yawning chasm between their ideal self (the self they wish to be and which they project to others) and their real self (the life they actually live). 'Shame' can be a crippling, dis-integrating condition for which people seek salvation. Whilst I do not concur with the entirety of Alan's diagnosis of the postmodern condition (see later) I do think that his comments on shame are very enlightening and can jolt us into seeing the world afresh. For this I am honestly grateful. We do need to address this issue of shame through the gospel narratives. The question 'How can a community help the chronically shamed person if the only narratives of healing and atonement they have to offer are ones based upon a reduction of sin and guilt to moral misdemeanour?' (Chapter 3) is indeed pertinent. I would add that the shame Alan identifies is often something *Christians* suffer with. We experience but often disguise the extent of the gap between an ideal self (the model Christian who exemplifies the fruit of the Spirit) and our real self. We can loath ourselves for constantly falling short of this ideal.

Alan's focus on the place of narrative is also important and his narrative account of conversion offers crucial insights. Again, whilst I feel that some of the claims for narrative are too strong, I do appreciate that it is central to Christian theology and a rich asset of our faith to exploit in a culture that is once again alive to the power of story. I found Alan's re-reading of the Passion Narratives and of Judas' story to be particularly interesting and genuinely 'revelatory'. These narratives really do have the power to engage with the issue of shame in ways that I had never seen before.

Having expressed some areas of appreciation and agreement I would like to raise some issues which I think require some clarification or modification.

Question 1: Is 'sin' a redundant concept?

Whilst acknowledging that 'sin' and 'guilt' are ideas which some people still find helpful in self-understanding,

Alan recommends dropping the *word* 'sin' because it is so overlaid with misunderstandings and rethinking the *concept* of sin by bringing biblical theology and our postmodern context into a dialogue. He writes, 'sin ... has become meaningless and insufficient as a descriptor for the plight of the postmodern self' (Chapter 1). He places 'shame' in the traditional role 'sin' inhabited as the plight from which we must be saved. I want to argue that whilst 'shame' is helpful to enable us to deepen and broaden our understanding of the human plight it should not serve as a substitute for sin even for those who are post-industrial, postmodern selves.

It is true that many do not feel troubled at having offended God but this is in large part because they are, to all intents and purposes, *de facto* atheists. Although many claim in public surveys to believe that some kind of 'God' exists, it is the case that for most people God is not on the radar of their day to day living. They lack, in other words, a Christian worldview. Now it will often be the case that one cannot immediately confront such people with their sin and their need to repent because such concepts will wash off them like water off a duck's back. Alan shows us that we need to take the route of listening to their *perceived* plight and showing how the gospel addresses it. But must we stop there? I worry that at times in the book it looks like Alan is suggesting that for some people we should. For instance, he says, 'It is therefore necessary to orientate our narratives of atonement so that they address the issues of shame, and not of 'sin' and guilt.' (Chapter 3) But why not *both*?

The Bible speaks of the amazing ability we humans have to deceive ourselves about our plight and it seems to me that to simply start *and end* with the *perceived* plight of postmodern people is to potentially capitulate to that capacity for self-deception. 'The post-industrialized self is *sinned against*, not sinner' (Chapter 11). But surely this is precisely the self-deception that needs unmasking! Let us just suppose that traditional claims about sin, guilt and our need of forgiveness are true. Then it is the case that we are sinners, we are guilty and we need to acknowledge that in repentance, *even if we do not perceive this existentially at a particular point in time*. There is a legitimate distinction to be made between our perceived plight and our plight, and one must not too easily conflate them.

Given that the loss of 'sin' in post-Christian culture is in large part due to the loss of God, would it not follow that the regaining of God through some kind of conversion (however sudden or gradual) would create the conditions for its recovery? Once God is scripted back into the narratives of our lives then it becomes meaningful again to imagine that one can offend against God and not merely our neighbour. Is not the missional challenge, in part at least, to try to reconnect the story that people tell about themselves to a Christian worldview? If this is so, as I believe it is, then whilst I am very happy to start by taking shame very seriously, I would not wish to avoid connecting it to more traditional Christian categories. Shame, I suggest, is to be seen as one of the manifestations of the brokenness of creation. It may not be the direct result of particular sins committed by the shamed person but neither is it unconnected to the web of human sin. Alan says at one point that the issue of shame must be dealt with *before* the issue of sin can become a meaningful concept. This more modest claim – that we need to take the long route rather than the shortcut – is helpful. To me it represents a positive way of appropriating his genuine insights.

I must confess that I think that even in a post-God, blame-shifting, victim-culture many people often do feel profound 'guilt' and a sense of moral failure. They do feel that, in principle at least, they are moral creatures with a responsibility for their choices and that the way that they treat the 'other' matters immensely. Alan's description of postmoderns as *pre*-moral (or post-moral?) does not resonate with my experience. The concept of 'shame' has not, or so it seems to me, *replaced* guilt so much as *supplemented* it. The concepts of forgiveness and moral transformation are not alien to people's felt needs even if the concept of *God's* forgiveness is less pressing. So here traditional theology still has routes in that it can stand alongside shame.

A final niggle: Alan speaks on several occasions of traditional notions of sin and contrasts them with the more postmodern notion of 'relational dysfunctionality'. It is the case that traditional notions are sometimes explained in non-interpersonal terms (e.g. breaking a moral rule) but when adequately explained traditional notions have always been about relational dys-functionality.

Question 2: Is divine judgement an unhelpful notion?

Postmodern people wish to be saved from *self*-judgement rather than *divine* judgement. This may indeed be the case but it is hard not to sympathise with those who say, 'Be that as it may, all must give account to God, and divine judgement is an issue which must be recognised at some point even if it is not an issue which troubles postmodern minds.' I realise that this is in some ways just a rehash of what I have already said, but let me just make this point: The notion of divine judgement (which is not simply to be reduced to God's punishment of sinners) is absolutely crucial to the portrayal of God right through the Old and New Testaments. To consider it as somehow optional is to potentially marginalize something *so dominant* in biblical faith that hard questions cannot avoid being asked. My own initial reflection is simply that I would like to accommodate Alan's notion of 'shame' within an understanding of that aspect of divine judgement that we call 'God's anger'. Could we not see 'shame' as in some ways analogous to God's giving people up to corruption as a manifestation of his wrath (Rom 1:18 ff)? On this account we situate shame within a Christian worldview as a manifestation of the results of the fall. It is a consequence of God's wrath understood as his allowing the cosmos to partially slip towards chaos. This allows us to link shame to judgement but also to acknowledge that it may not be the particular sins of the one who is shamed which led to the condition. Whilst this may not be something one would confront a non-Christian with for reasons already explained, it allows Christians to do justice to biblical revelation and Alan's helpful insights.

Question 3: How important is the *historical* truth of the gospel narrative into which we weave our own stories?

Alan says that a 'storied approach to the atonement … is more likely to engage the postmodern with its meaning. This is because, firstly, it comes to them in a recognizable and less threatening manner and, secondly, because it professes to do no more than other narratives that are heard via therapy, novel, film or cyberspace – to live in the world they create *as if* it is the real world' (italics mine). But what exactly does this 'as if' amount to? Does it mean that I may say, 'Well I don't believe that Jesus really is the Saviour of the world but I choose to live *as if* he were'? Presumably not. Yet the comment that the narrative account of atonement 'professes to do no more than narratives that are heard via ... novel, [or] film ...' does raise concerns. The kind of truth that novels or films convey does not (usually) depend on the content of those stories matching up with actual historical people or events. It would not matter one iota to the impact of a film like *The Shawshank Redemption* whether Andy Dufresne (Tim Robbins' character) actually existed or not. To live *as if* this narrative is true means something other than living *as if* Andy Dufresne existed and did the things portrayed in the film. It is rather to live in the world *as if* the values and human possibilities embodied in the film were ones one also sought to live by. Can we say the same about the gospels? Yes and no. Of course, one could benefit from reading the gospels simply at the level of stories without believing that Jesus even existed. But is the call to discipleship and salvation simply a call to embrace the ideals and human possibilities of a fictional character? Hardly! Let me provide an analogy.

Suppose that you are locked in a prison and that someone comes and tells you the story of a fellow prisoner who earlier in the day had unlocked the prison door so that those inside could escape. To live as if *this* story is true is to walk up to the prison door and try to open it. But, of course, if the story is *not* true then living as if it were will do little good because the door will remain closed. In *this* kind of story, states of affairs in the real world do matter. Christians have always claimed that the story of the gospel and of the atonement is more like this prison story than like *The Shawshank Redemption* or *Pride and Prejudice*. It matters that Jesus really existed, really did the Father's works, really died and was really resurrected. The call to cohabit with this narrative is the call to accept that this narrative is true and to live accordingly. The *as if* is fine though somewhat redundant here – no more than a comment to the effect that, 'Of course, I may be mistaken but here I stand.'

I am sure that Alan would agree with all this, so what I am asking for is clarification. At times he seems to make radical claims such as the following: 'it would seem self-evident that the Christian faith is *nothing more than* (though vitally nothing less than) one story among an infinite number of other stories' (Chapter Six, italics mine). The 'nothing more than' seems worryingly reductionist, however, I think that it should be interpreted as a preacher's over-statement. He explains later that: 'Though *in the end* it becomes clear that the Christian (meta)narrative makes unique claims upon truth, upon history, upon humanity and the origin and end of life, in its *initial* encounter with the self it should assert nothing more than the right to be heard, to be considered along with the polyphony of other voices, of other narratives that collide and conflict with any given individual or community' (Chapter Six, italics mine). This is helpful and provides genuinely useful missional advice. What I would like further help with is in under-standing *why* the historicity of the story matters. Could not a *fictional* story provide the kind of counter-narrative postmoderns seek? If so could Alan's atonement theology survive with a fictional Jesus? Also could it allow other fictional saviours to co-exist with Jesus so long as they achieve the goal of calling shamed people towards lives lived in freedom from shame? These are important questions.

Is the cross necessary?

The saving power of the atonement narratives for Alan seems to lie in this fact: that there was no gap between Jesus' lived life and his ideal self revealed at the Last Supper. This opens up the possibility that we, who shamefully fall far short of the ideals we set for ourselves, can find redemption. As I said earlier, I do think that this is a very helpful way of thinking. So long as one does not think that this exhausts what atonement is about (and Alan would never claim that it does) I have no problems with it at all. However, I feel in need of some clarification.

For Alan, Jesus is salvific for the shamed because his story opens up the imaginative possibility of living in a similar non-shameful way. This saves postmodern selves by calling them to pick up their crosses and walk in the same way. But why must *Jesus* be the Saviour? Could not the Moses (or some other) character provide all the coherence between ideal self and real self that we need for atonement?

Was Jesus' *divinity* important for the atoning power of his story or is his humanity enough? Indeed is *God* necessary for the story to have healing power for the shamed self? Could a humanist version do the trick? I am sure Alan would answer that Christ's deity and the Father's role are crucial but I still feel in need of some clarification as to *why* they should be.

Is there a danger that one could see *the story itself*, rather than God, as having saving power? Is conversion *no more than* retelling our story differently? I don't think Alan would answer with a 'yes' but I worry that some could read his work in that way. As Kevin Vanhoozer asks of Paul Ricoeur's narrative philosophy, 'can the imagination free us from the bondage indicated by the symbols of evil and the doctrine of sin? ... Is regeneration really a matter of refiguring the imagination?' (*Biblical Narrative in the Philosophy of Paul Ricoeur: a Study in Hermeneutics and Theology*, Cambridge University Press, 1990, pp. 240, 247). Vanhoozer says that for Christians there are three conditions for salvation – the historical deed of God in Christ which forms the foundation of the possible, the poetic word in Scripture which proclaims the deed, and the Spirit which is the power that appropriates the word of *kerygma.* Now Alan's concluding comments make some excellent qualifications of his argument by emphasising the place of the resurrection and the Spirit. It is a shame that these are not more prominent in the main body of the book because they would guard against the possible misreading of his theology identified above.

And why did Jesus have to die? Could he not have simply narrated a purpose for himself according to which he came to serve others, and then done so without ever dying (after all, one can serve others without dying for them)? Would *that* have been sufficient for atonement? I think that Alan would say that Jesus' death is crucial because it represents a sharing in the relationally dehumanizing condition of the shamed 'self'. Ironically, in his being publicly 'shamed' on the cross, he lived and died as the one without the 'shame' of an incoherent self. Thus he 'absorbs the relational dysfunction of others' (Chapter 9). It is in Chapter 9 that Alan comes closest to explaining why Jesus' death is so central and necessary to atone for the shamed and yet I still feel somewhat unclear on the above issues.

Alan's book is a most stimulating and original piece of Christian theology. I do offer the above comments and questions not as disproof of his account of the atonement, but merely as initial requests for further reflection and clarification. There may well be straightforward answers to some of my questions and I would encourage Alan and his 'fans' to pursue his model further to see how well it can deal with the questions and situate itself in relation to more traditional theology. I would however, urge them to walk cautiously and to beware of throwing out beautiful babies with the muddy bathwater.

We all know where we are coming from, but do we know where we are going? A response to Robin Parry

Alan Mann

If you are reading this in the year 2010 (or even 2006 for that matter!), you may be blissfully unaware that this book was published at a time when there was much debate, particularly among evangelical Christians, as to what could, should and absolutely must not be said about the atonement. Though another book I was involved in at the time was partly responsible for this debate, the appearance of this particular treatise on the atonement was never intended to be part of such pro-ceedings. Given that the original argument that formed the foundation of this book was an MA thesis I wrote back in 1999–2000, and that this particular manuscript was finished months before any whiff of debate hung in the air, I hope that the reader will be satisfied that it is not some crass attempt to make money and mileage from the theological flavour of the month. That it is about the atonement is pure coincidence without even a smattering of intent. The only bandwagon I hope to have jumped on is one ridden by those who desire to make meaningful the life, death and resurrection of Jesus for their own time and place. In any case, whether such coincidence will prove fortuitous or fatal for this book is unknown to me at this point.

I tell you this because I think it helps to explain why there is a dialogue at the back of this book. On balance, this is not common procedure, unless the clear purpose of a book is to have a dialogue on a certain issue or topic. Indeed, when Paternoster approached me to ask if I would consider this, I had my reservations. Why do such a thing? After all, there are books in print that are far more theologically controversial than the one you hold in your hands, which make no apology or qualification of their content. Was I being asked to clarify my argument for the less careful reader? Or was this a necessary exercise to placate those who would have reservations about my theology or concerns about my agenda. While it may serve this purpose, this is not the reason for this addendum. In any case, as I have already stated at the beginning of the book, I am unable to please all Christians, all of the time, no matter how I construe my views on the atonement. Rather, the dialogue found here is an opportunity to reiterate the fact that this book is not a credo but an invitation to take seriously the implication emerging cultures have for our missional methodology, and how this phenomenon can render inadequate the 'vehicle' we use to communicate the gospel, even if it cannot place into question the truth of the gospel itself.

All this is a digression, even if it is a helpful one, for the purpose here is to dialogue with some concerns and criticisms of what has been said in the main body of the text. In some senses, I am being asked to qualify certain points. However, while I am happy to do this, all concerned with this dialogue need to keep in mind that qualification can end in a never ending spiral that has the very real danger of losing the purpose or reason for writing in the first place – and that I consciously choose to avoid, as already indicated in the introduction of the book.

Teetering on the edge of tradition

A common thread in Robin's critique is that he feels I overreach myself, in my diagnosis of the postmodern condition or my claims for narrative, to name but two. This is a criticism I am willing to stand. Indeed, I am grateful that in overreaching, some (like Robin) are willing to catch me rather than give me the final push over the edge. However, in my flippancy, there is a serious point to be made. I make no secret of the fact that I am overreaching myself, for this serves a purpose. In order to catch me, Robin has had to follow me into my argument. He has had to consider seriously my ideas, my thoughts and my challenges. Though he may have 'saved' me from more serious error, he is no longer standing as far back from my position as he once was. However, I too have not strayed as far away from theological tradition as he may have feared. Through open dialogue we are finding (notice I am not suggesting we have found) common ground and a common purpose. Though my printed words cannot be changed, my theological thoughts surrounding the atonement and how it engages with the context I find myself in are always fluid. This book is written for the purpose of dialogue and not for the creation of 'theological-stones' with which to attack those who disagree with me. Personally speaking, I would rather be rebuked, as Peter was by our Lord, for enthusiastically overreaching myself from time-to-time, than remain safely behind theological walls that others have put around me while my cultural peers remain lost in a story that has a major plot line missing.

A 'shame' to be misunderstood

One of the most fascinating insights this dialogue has thrown up is how easily one can be misunderstood even when one feels that they have been so careful and measured in the way the argument is rendered. This is no more evident than in Robin's first question about the redundancy of the concept of sin.

While I do suggest we stop using the *word* 'sin', this is not the same as dropping the *concept*. I am not the first to suggest that the word 'sin' within the biblical canon, and therefore within our own culture, has a wide semantic domain that encompasses far more than we typically allow for within our contemporary expressions of atonement. Therefore, Robin has misunderstood when he suggests that I have placed 'shame' in the traditional role of 'sin' and guilt, for shame does not replace sin, but is merely a condition that should be seen to be within the semantic domain of sin because it is a perceived plight of the postmodern that Jesus deals with at Calvary. Indeed, the only clear definition of 'sin' that I use (and I use it *ad nauseam*) describes it thus: the *absence* of mutual, undistorted, unpolluted relating.

Obviously, I have been too subtle in making my point here. What I am trying to suggest by constantly placing inverted commas around the word 'sin', is that we employ this word as though it meaningfully describes the condition of all, when in fact it encompasses a myriad of human conditions that need atoning. Due to a semantic reduction, sin (which encompasses guilt) has come to be associated *only* with guilt. Therefore, in a 'sinless' society, where guilt is a concept that has lost much of its ability to stick to the human psyche, the word sin (which is inextricably associated with guilt) has lost its ability to draw people to Jesus, to be atoned for, forgiven and healed.

Perhaps it would be helpful to illustrate this metaphorically. Imagine we are able to take a photograph of all that sin encompasses. In order to frame the photograph we may choose to have a focal point. However, in making such a decision, much of the rest of the photograph can be thrown out of focus. It is not absent, it is still part of the picture, still within its borders, but it has become part of the background while our subject takes the dominant role and draws our immediate attention.

What I am suggesting is that in the postmodern, post-industrialised 'photograph' of 'sin', the subject may well be 'shame', or 'anxiety', or 'ontological incoherence'. Guilt is still present, but it is out of focus. It may well become an issue at a later stage in the process, but is not the primary condition, nor the perceived plight of the postmodern that will unlock for them the need for a 'saving' encounter with the story of atonement.

Unfortunately, my use of the word 'perception' has also proved a stumbling block for Robin's understanding. Perhaps it would reassure all readers to say that, perception is not something felt that has a form of unreality. We perceive something to be so because it is very real – and it is from reality that we need saving. In fact, perception serves as an added critique, for *to perceive* is to notice or discern something that others have failed to do. In our context, the discerned plight *is* 'shame', 'anxiety', 'lostness', an 'inability to trust' or 'ontological incoherence' and yet too often we fail postmodern people by simply demanding their condition *be* one of guilt. This is not the same as denying that guilt is part of the human condition. Rather, I am suggesting that, even allowing for this, a guilt-based model of atonement is not the only, nor necessarily the most fruitful model in a postmodern, post-industrialised increasingly therapeutic context.

A matter of sound judgement

I largely found Robin's input on the issue of divine wrath and judgement perfectly reasonable and helpful, particularly in his analogy of God's wrath as something that allows the cosmos to partially slip towards chaos. I'm sure though that Robin is fully aware (as I am) that all this seems a little too passive on God's part for many people's understanding of God's role in judgment. It may please Robin, and others, to know that, despite the fact I talk throughout the book about the role of non-judgement in reconciliation, I am happy to concur with him that 'divine judgement is an issue that must be recognised ... even if it is not an issue which troubles postmodern minds.' Though I still hold to my position that Jesus, like the father in the Prodigal Son, is looking for restoration and reconciliation without judgement, this cannot and should not dissuade us from the fact that the atonement and God's judgement go hand in hand.

Elsewhere, I have been criticised, along with Steve Chalke, for emphasising the love of God so as to deny God's wrath. For some, I have ignored the obvious biblical understanding that crucifixion, with all its pain and injury, torture and terror should be my lot as a sinner, but that it has to be borne instead by Jesus. Though I know it is likely to further offend my critics, I have to say that I find this an unnecessary and distorted understanding of the biblical revelation and for good reason.

I believe the cross graphically symbolises that which is beyond comprehension (our separation from God) rather than a space/time demonstration to us of our literal fate as sinners in the hands of an angry God. For if it cannot be seen that to face 'death' (physically and metaphorically) and so 'live' with the reality of separation from God (from divine parental love) for eternity, is not all the 'wrath' and judgement any one person could stand, then I truly fear for our understanding of the Christian faith. Faced with this torment (and let it be understood that this is suggestive of person to person, as well as human/divine relating) other threats of tortuous punishments pale by comparison.

Again, like sin, my fear is that wrath has become a misused and misunderstood term and should be used sparingly if it is to maintain a biblical and meaningful purpose for the postmodern. To that end, I would suggest here that there are few who would fail to grasp the weight and tragedy of facing an eternal separation by death from all those we love and who love us. That Jesus is able and willing to alter this emotionally, physically and spiritually by 'punishing torment', is truly good news.

A brief history of truth

There are myriad reasons why I chose to emphasise narrative or story as the methodology by which we should approach the postmodern with the atonement, which I do not need to repeat here. Though critical of how I at times handle this preference, Robin's critique also serves to re-emphasise the fruitfulness of story in our context.

Though I am not dismissing some of the valuable issues Robin raises here, indeed I continue to wrestle with them, it would be hard to answer them briefly with any sense of satisfaction, for they touch on profound issues of epistemology and the nature of reality and truth. To answer the question, 'How important is historical truth?' raises the equally valid retort, 'That depends on what you understand by the term, "historical truth"'. It is a moot point, but I would suggest that what modernity means by history and how such a concept is used to speak of truth, is not necessarily in continuity with the purposes of the gospels, even if such a statement raises more questions than it answers. Furthermore, historians are apt at demonstrating that history itself is a phenomenon no less subject to interpretation than any narrative, which make statements of fact, truth or meaning derived from it, very nebulous. Therefore, I choose to stand by my statement that, the Christian faith (or indeed the gospels themselves) are nothing more than (though vitally nothing less than) one story among many. For even though 'nothing more than' sounds 'worryingly reductionist' its corollary, 'nothing *less* than' does more than simply neutralise such a statement. For even though it is not necessary for propositional statements or appeals to fact to have one, restrictive interpretation, they are often employed in this way, particularly in the dogmatism of religious expression. Story, on the other hand (and I include the gospel in this), has what I would argue is the advantage of polyvalence, which allows it to mean different things to different people, or even different things to the same person depending on their circumstance. However, as anyone who has the most superficial knowledge of literary theory will tell you (and

I would probably include myself in this category) this does not automatically imply that we can make what we will from a text. It may have many meanings, but that is not the same as saying that it has endless meanings. But as you can see, we wander deeper into the realms of philosophy, epistemology and literary criticism, and I do not necessarily have the 'light' to take the reader into such dark places, so I will turn back here, even if it leaves the more adventurous reader disappointed and unsatisfied.

Are we really at cross-purposes?

Was the cross necessary? Was Jesus' divinity important for the atonement? Is God necessary for the story to have healing power? Robin's final barrage of questions deserves protracted, theologically erudite and biblically sustained answers. And yet I feel the need to simply reply with a most emphatic, unsubstantiated, faith-driven, 'YES!', allowing me a respite so that I may go and ponder these further, knowing full well that here, more than anywhere else, our human finiteness needs the spiritual balm of mystery. However, for the sake of entering into this dialogue, I will endeavour to reach from the finite into the infinite, even if the accusation may be raised yet again, that I am overreaching myself.

If I have come close to answering any of Robin's questions already, then it is perhaps the question of why Jesus had to die, and by implication, was the cross necessary. As Robin himself indicates, Chapter 9 of the book deals with these issues at length (though pockets of other chapters also touch on this topic). Though he expresses concerns about the clarity with which I do this, I would suggest that the modern disease, lack of time, brought upon both of us by publishing deadlines, is as much to blame for his dissatisfaction as my inability to express myself. Indeed, I would want to suggest that if any reader were to take these questions and concerns back to the main body of the text, they would be as satisfied with the answers they find there than with any subsequent input I may give here.

As for the question of the necessity of Jesus' divinity, I would wish to make a couple of points. Firstly, though the question relates to arguments about the atonement put forward in this book, I was minded to ask this same question of the way other models of atonement are typically described. Is it always obvious from our accounts of penal substitution (to take the most commonly adopted model of atonement), that Jesus had to be divine in order to satisfy the demands of God? In my experience, the answer is most probably, no. Though I am sure if the question was asked an answer would be given, even if it was not necessarily always a satisfactory one. But this is becoming an evasive tactic. The question is not being asked of penal substitution but of atonement for a 'sinless' society. Let me kill two birds with one stone, for they are standing close together.

Robin asks, 'Could not the Moses (or some other) character provide all the coherence between ideal self and real self that we need for atonement?' Here, I shall let a friend answer, for in reading Robin's question for herself she answered without hesitation, 'No, because Moses was not coherent. No person has ever been ontologically coherent.' All have fallen short of God's glory, of what God intended for humanity at our inception. To deepen the answer, yet without detracting from its profound simplicity, only in the divine, *perichoretic union* of Father, Son and Holy Spirit do we find such coherence – or in other words, the absence of 'sin' (that being the *presence* of mutual, undistorted unpolluted relating). Post-Fall (though it was, and should still be a vital expression of what it means to be made human in the image of God), the only place we find ontological coherence is in the divine. Post-Calvary (or more accurately, post-resurrection), the hope of an ontologically, and narratively-coherent humanity, has been restored.

This may not satisfy all (and may not ultimately satisfy me as an argument) so I continue to wrestle with this question, not only for my arguments in this book, but in all the ways I choose to express the atoning work of Christ. However, for now, it serves two purposes: it gives an answer that is in continuity with the issues raised in the book, and it keeps open the dialogue, so that we may all move to more satisfactory answers.

An inevitable end

While I was in the process of writing the manuscript for this book a professor of theology questioned whether it would ever see the light of day. The basis for his doubt lay in the fact that in his own experience it was easy enough to find a Christian publisher who was willing to put in print something that had already been said a hundred times before. Far harder was it to find a publisher who would take on a project that had something new and insightful to say – risking criticism or even ridicule for doing so. To that end, I would like to take this opportunity to thank Paternoster for being a publisher with genuine theological and missiological concern, who, despite some reservations, typical of the ones expressed by Robin, could see past them and come to understand and value the contribution such radically orthodox thinking has to play in reaching an emerging culture with a message of 'good news'.

Finally, I would like to observe that, though not a typical procedure, I have enjoyed, been stimulated by and valued the opportunity for dialogue, even before the book has gone to press. Though all writing inevitably ends with a full-stop, it is hoped that these few pages of dialogue indicate that theology is 'faith seeking understanding' and is, therefore, part of the ongoing question 'what does it mean to be a follower of Christ?' To that end, theology should never be an untouchable, propositional statement, but always open to dialogue, therefore . . .

Notes

1. S. TeSelle, *Speaking in Parables* (London: SCM Press, 1975), 1.
2. J.B. Green and M.D. Baker, *Recovering the Scandal of the Cross* (Carlisle: Paternoster/Downers Grove: IVP, 2000), 18.
3. Green and Baker, *Recovering*, 12, 13.
4. D.J. Hall, *The Cross in Our Context* (Minneapolis: Fortress Press, 2003), 130.
5. E. Becker, *The Denial of Death* (New York: Free Press, 1973), 198.
6. J. Bowker, *The Meaning of Death* (Cambridge: Cambridge University Press, 1991), 97–98. Cited by J. Sankey, 'With, Through and in Christ: A Eucharist Approach to Atonement', in *Atonement Today* (ed.) J. Goldingay (London: SPCK, 1995).
7. Bryan Appleyard, 'Is Sin Good?', *The Sunday Times Magazine* (11 April 2004), 18–28 (p. 20).
8. Appleyard, 'Is Sin Good?', 20.
9. Elements of the historical development of 'the self' can be found in works such as Becker, *Denial* and A. Giddens, *Modernity and Self Identity* (Cambridge: Polity Press, 1991).
10. Hall, *Cross*, 104.
11. Hall, *Cross*, 104.

12. R. Lundin, *The Culture of Interpretation* (Grand Rapids: Eerdmans, 1993), 75.

13. J.R. Middleton and B.J. Walsh, *Truth Is Stranger than It Used to Be* (London: SPCK, 1995), 59.

14. C.M. Gay, *The Way of the (Modern) World* (Grand Rapids: Eerdmans, 1998), 193.

15. R. R. Ruether, *Introducing Redemption in Christian Feminism* (Sheffield: Sheffield Academic Press, 1998), 72.

16. D. Coupland, *Life after God* (London: Simon & Schuster, 1995), 273.

17. C. Lasch, *The Culture of Narcissism* (New York: W.W. Norton, 1991), 6.

18. W. Brueggemann, *The Covenanted Self* (Minneapolis: Fortress Press, 1999), 23.

19. K. Carmichael, *Sin and Forgiveness: New Responses in a Changing World* (Aldershot: Ashgate, 2003), xxi.

20. Meic Pearse, *Why the Rest Hates the West: Understanding the Roots of Global Rage* (London: SPCK, 2003), 59.

21. Pearse, *Why*, 64.

22. Pearse, *Why*, 78.

23. J. Humphrys, *Devil's Advocate* (London: Arrow Books, 2000), 9.

24. J. Fletcher, 'Sin in Contemporary Literature', *Theology Today* 50.2 (1993), 254–64 (p. 254).

25. *Good Will Hunting* (London: Miramax Films and Buena Vista Home Entertainment, 1997).

26. L.G. Jones, *Embodying Forgiveness: A Theological Analysis* (Grand Rapids: Eerdmans, 1995), 46.

27. Jones, *Embodying*, 116.

28. Green and Baker, *Recovering*, 92.

29. Gay, *The Way*, 187.

30. Appleyard, 'Is Sin Good?', 22.

31. Lasch, *Narcissism*, 7.

32. J. Fowler, *Faithful Change* (Nashville: Abingdon Press, 1996), 91. Cited by S. Pattison, *Shame: Theory, Therapy, Theology* (Cambridge: Cambridge University Press, 2000), 1.

33. J. Bradshaw, *Healing the Shame that Binds You* (Deerfield Beach: Heath Communications Inc., 1988).

34. G. Kaufman, *Shame: The Power of Caring* (Rochester: Shenkman Books, 1985), ix–x.
35. Pattison, *Shame*, 76. These terms are used extensively throughout Professor Stephen Pattison's book. In my opinion this is the most comprehensive work to date on the subject and has influenced much that is said here regarding the issue of shame.
36. Selected quotations from Pattison, *Shame*, 70.
37. Pattison, *Shame*, 42.
38. Giddens, *Modernity*, 172.
39. Coupland, *Life*, 145.
40. Pattison, *Shame*, 73.
41. See D. Capps, *The Depleted Self: Sin in a Narcissistic Age* (Minneapolis: Fortress Press, 1993), 72.
42. A. Ball, *American Beauty* (London: FilmFour Books, 1999), 21.
43. Pattison, *Shame*, 76.
44. Pattison, *Shame*, 77.
45. Capps, *Depleted*, 7.
46. Pattison, *Shame*, 73.
47. Pattison, *Shame*, 167.
48. Pattison, *Shame*, 143.
49. Pattison, *Shame*, 74.
50. G. Kaufman and L. Raphael, *Coming Out of Shame: Transforming Gay and Lesbian Lives* (New York: Doubleday, 1996), 179.
51. Pattison, *Shame*, 76.
52. Barefoot Doctor, 'The Shame Game', *Observer Magazine* (11 July 2004), 58. For the uninitiated, Barefoot Doctor is an alternative health, spirituality and lifestyle guru. As well as writing a weekly column for the *Observer Magazine* he is the author of several best-selling self-help books and a regular broadcaster. With website hits registering in the millions, his influence is without question.
53. Kaufman and Raphael, *Coming Out*, 110.
54. Pattison, *Shame*, 156.
55. Green and Baker, *Recovering*, 201.
56. Pattison, *Shame*, 88.

57. Pattison, *Shame*, 123.
58. Certainly, for example, I struggled to understand my need to pray the sinner's prayer as a seventeen-year-old, because I couldn't see what I had *done* wrong. However, I had a deep desire to follow Jesus because I could grasp that truth and life were found in him. Only later did I begin to understand and feel my sinfulness as a human being.
59. Pattison, *Shame*, 289.
60. Capps, *Depleted*, 83.
61. Pattison, *Shame*, 90.
62. C. Goldberg, *Understanding Shame* (Northvale: Jason Aronson, 1991), 257. Cited by Pattison, *Shame*, 169.
63. Hall, *Cross*, 132.
64. P. Sherry, *Images of Redemption* (London: T&T Clark, 2003), 107.
65. B. Hardy, 'Towards a Poetics of Fiction: An Approach through Narrative', *Novel* 2 (1968), 5–14 (p. 5). Cited in A. MacIntyre, *After Virtue* (Notre Dame: Notre Dame University Press, 1981), 211.
66. P. Cobley, *Narrative* (London: Routledge, 2003), 2.
67. S. Crites, 'The Narrative Quality of Experience', in *Why Narrative? Readings in Narrative Theology* (ed.) S. Hauerwas and G.L. Jones (Grand Rapids: Eerdmans, 1989), 66-88 (p. 69).
68. G. Loughlin, *Telling God's Story: Bible, Church, and Narrative Theology* (Cambridge: Cambridge University Press, 1996), 142.
69. E.O. Wilson, 'Wings across Two Cultures', *The Guardian: Saturday Review* (8 June 2000), 4. In this article, Wilson discusses the challenge and benefits of combining science and literature.
70. S. Grenz and R.E. Olson, *Twentieth-century Theology* (Carlisle: Paternoster, 1992), 277.
71. G. Fackre, 'Narrative Theology: An Overview', *Interpretation* 37 (1983), 340-52 (p. 341).
72. S.W. Sykes, 'Story and Eucharist', *Interpretation* 37 (1983), 365-36 (p. 366).

73. Becker, *Denial*, 3.
74. M. Payne, *Narrative Therapy* (London: SAGE Publications, 2000), 20.
75. Loughlin, *Telling*, 9.
76. K. B. Jensen, *The Social Semiotics of Mass Communication* (London: SAGE Publications, 1995), 11.
77. W. Brueggemann, *The Bible and Postmodern Imagination* (London: SCM Press, 1993), 70.
78. Brueggemann, *Imagination*, 20.
79. Giddens, *Modernity*, 190.
80. A. Parry and R.E. Doan, *Story Re-Visions: Narrative Therapy in the Postmodern World*, (New York: Guildford Press, 1994), 1.
81. A. Wilder, 'Story and Story-World', *Interpretation* 37 (1983), 353-64 (p. 362).
82. Parry and Doan, *Story*, 5.
83. R. Williams, *Lost Icons: Reflections on Cultural Bereavement* (Edinburgh: T&T Clark, 2000), 144.
84. E. Robinson, *The Language of Mystery* (London: SCM Press, 1987), 8.
85. J. McLeod, *Narrative and Psychotherapy* (London: SAGE Publications, 1997), 26.
86. G.W. Stroup, *The Promise of Narrative Theology* (London: SCM Press, 1984), 111.
87. Pattison, *Shame*, 144.
88. Based on the work of A. Morgan, *What Is Narrative Therapy?* (Adelaide: Dulwich Centre Publications, 2000), 46.
89. Parry and Doan, *Story*, 5, 6.
90. Pattison, *Shame*, 169.
91. Gianfranco Ceccin, 'Address to Association for Family Therapy', *Context* 8.4. Cited by Payne, *Narrative*, 45.
92. McLeod, *Narrative*, 26.
93. Payne, *Narrative*, 85.
94. Morgan, *Therapy*, 15.
95. Parry and Doan, *Story*, 30, 31.
96. MacIntyre, *Virtue*, 218.
97. E. Levinas E. and R. Kearney, 'Dialogue with Emmanuel

Levinas', in *Face to Face with Levinas* (ed.) R.A. Cohen (Albany: State University of New York Press, 1986). Cited by Parry and Doan, *Story*, 31–32.

98. Stroup, *Promise*, 129.
99. A.C. Thiselton, *Interpreting God and the Postmodern Self* (Edinburgh: T&T Clark, 1995), 76. Author's italics.
100. Stroup, *Promise*, 247.
101. Goldingay, *Models for Scripture* (Carlisle: Paternoster, 1987), 65.
102. Stroup, *Promise*, 116.
103. M. Root, 'The Narrative Structure of Soteriology', *Modern Theology* 2.2 (1986), 145-59 (p. 146).
104. M. Grey, *Redeeming the Dream: Feminism, Redemption and Christian Tradition* (London: SPCK, 1989), 126.
105. Pattison, *Shame*, 247.
106. Loughlin, *Telling*, 21.
107. M. Buber, *I and Thou* (Edinburgh: T&T Clark, 1958), 18. Cited by, Grey, *Redeeming*, 85.
108. Hall, *Cross*, 104.
109. Hall, *Cross*, 128.
110. Brueggemann, *Imagination*, 21, 25.
111. Green and Baker, *Recovering*, 110.
112. Goldingay, *Models*, 67.
113. Stroup, *Promise*, 190.
114. B.F. Meyer, *The Aims of Jesus* (London: SCM Press, 1979), 218.
115. H.W. Frei, 'Theological Reflections on the Accounts of Jesus' Death and Resurrection', in *Hans Frei: Theology and Narrative: Selected Essays* (ed. G. Hunsinger and W. Placher; Oxford: Oxford University Press, 1993), 74.
116. Loughlin, *Telling*, 156.
117. G. Green, *Imagining God: Theology and the Religious Imagination* (Grand Rapids: Eerdmans, 1989), 147.
118. H.U. Balthasar, *Mysterium Paschale* (Edinburgh: T&T Clark, 1990), 96.
119. Loughlin, *Telling*, 223.
120. D. Senior, *The Passion of Jesus in the Gospel of Mark* (Wilmington: Glazier, 1984), 59.

121. Frei, 'Reflections', 57.
122. J. Kodell, *The Eucharist in the New Testament* (Wilmington: Glazier, 1988), 91.
123. J.B. Green, *The Gospel of Luke* (Grand Rapids: Eerdmans, 1997), 762.
124. B. Thorne, *Person-centred Counselling and Christian Spirituality: The Secular and the Holy* (London: Whurr Publishers, 2000), 26.
125. Thorne, *Counselling*, 26.
126. Loughlin, *Telling*, 74.
127. Hall, *Cross*, 40.
128. Balthasar, *Mysterium*, 105. See also Green, *Luke*, 777: 'On the Mount of Olives Jesus prayerfully declares his fundamental orientation around the will of God; if this leads to calamity and death, so be it.'
129. Grey, *Redeeming*, 95.
130. D. Rhoades and D. Michie, *Mark as Story* (Philadelphia: Fortress Press, 1982), 113.
131. Frei, 'Reflections', 56.
132. K.T. Hughes, 'Framing Judas', *Semeia* 54 (1991), 223-31 (p. 225).
133. Pattison, *Shame*, 128.
134. Senior, *Passion*, 52.
135. Senior, *Passion*, 53.
136. Green, *Luke*, 764.
137. Senior, *Passion*, 53.
138. Thorne, *Counselling*, 26.
139. V. Brümmer, *The Model of Love* (Cambridge: Cambridge University Press, 1993), 197.
140. C.F. Whelan, 'Suicide in the Ancient World: A Re-Examination of Matt 27:3–10', *Laval Théologique et Philosophique* 49 (1993), 505–22 (p. 519). Cited by W. Klassen, *Judas: Betrayer or Friend of Jesus?* (London: SCM Press, 1996), 166.
141. MacIntyre, *Virtue*, 217.
142. Thorne, *Counselling*, 27.
143. Kodell, *Eucharist*, 90.
144. Rhoades and Michie, *Mark*, 128.
145. Thorne, *Counselling*, 26.

146. Thorne, *Counselling*, 35.

147. Hall, *Cross*, 38.

148. Thorne, *Counselling*, 23.

149. Hall, *Cross*, 91.

150. J. Kingsbury, *Matthew as Story* (Philadelphia: Fortress Press, 1988), 89.

151. Balthasar, *Mysterium*, 109.

152. Frei, 'Reflections', 62.

153. Rhoades and Michie, *Mark*, 112.

154. Pattison, *Shame*, 183.

155. Rhoades and Michie, *Mark*, 115.

156. R.C. Tannehill, *Luke* (Nashville: Abingdon Press, 1996), 343.

157. Thorne, *Counselling*, 22.

158. J. Patton, *Is Human Forgiveness Possible? A Pastoral Care Perspective* (Lima: Academic Renewal Press, 2003), 55.

159. C. Gestrich, *The Return of Splendor in the World* (Grand Rapids: Eerdmans, 1997), 291.

160. Morgan, *Therapy*, 111.

161. See, for example, the discussion in Green, *Luke* (note especially his footnotes 6, 7 and 8 on p. 843).

162. A. Walker, *Telling the Story* (London: SPCK, 1996), 196.

163. K. Leach, *The Sky is Red: Discerning the Signs of the Times* (London: Darton, Longman and Todd, 1997), 164.

164. Sankey, 'With, Through, and in Christ', 93.

165. D.E. Smith and H.E. Taussig, *Many Tables: The Eucharist in the New Testament and Liturgy Today* (London: SCM Press, 1990), 19.

166. See Smith and Taussig, *Many Tables*.

167. T. Gorringe, *The Signs of Love: Reflections on the Eucharist* (London: SPCK, 1997), 15.

168. Pattison, *Shame*, 160.

169. Pattison, *Shame*, 76.

170. Sykes, 'Story', 372.

171. Gestrich, *Return*, 47. Drawing on Nietzsche's *On the Genealogy of Morality*.

172. For a full account of the ideas surrounding this narrative see W.H. Willomon, 'A Peculiarly Christian Account of Sin', *Theology Today* 50.2 (1993), 220–28.

173. Willomon, 'Account', 221.

174. Gestrich, *Return*, 177.

175. Willomon, 'Account', 227.

176. Jim Cotter, *Prayer in the Morning* (Exeter: Jim Cotter, 1987), 3. Cited by Pattison, *Shame*, 301.

177. Stroup, *Promise*, 170.

178. Gorringe, *Signs*, 25.

179. Stroup, *Promise*, 212.

180. S. Richards, 'Doing the Story: Narrative, Mission and Eucharist', in *Mass Culture: Eucharist and Mission in a Post-Modern World* (ed.) P. Ward (Oxford: Bible Reading Fellowship, 1999), 126.

181. Pattison, *Shame*, 160.

182. M. Volf, *Exclusion and Embrace: A Theological Exploration of Identity, Otherness, and Reconciliation* (Nashville: Abingdon Press, 1996), 129

183. Volf, *Exclusion*, 129.

184. Loughlin, *Telling*, 214.

185. C.E. Gunton, *The Actuality of Atonement* (Edinburgh: T&T Clark, 1988), 175.

186. Loughlin, *Telling*, 163.

187. Thiselton, *Interpreting God*, 78.

188. Stroup, *Promise*, 243.

189. Gunton, *Actuality*, 167.

190. Thiselton, *Interpreting God*, 160.

191. Brümmer, *Model*, 200.

Bibliography

Appleyard, B., 'Is Sin Good?', *The Sunday Times Magazine* (11 April 2004), 18–28.

Ball, A., *American Beauty* (London: FilmFour Books, 1999).

Balthasar, H.U., *Mysterium Paschale* (Edinburgh: T&T Clark, 1990).

Barefoot Doctor, 'The Shame Game', *Observer Magazine* (11 July 2004).

Becker, E., *The Denial of Death* (New York: Free Press, 1973).

Bowker, J., *The Meaning of Death* (Cambridge: Cambridge University Press, 1991).

Bradshaw, J., *Healing the Shame that Binds You* (Deerfield Beach: Heath Communications Inc., 1988).

Brueggemann, W., *The Bible and Postmodern Imagination* (London: SCM Press, 1993).

—, *The Covenanted Self* (Minneapolis: Fortress Press, 1999).

Brümmer, V., *The Model of Love* (Cambridge: Cambridge University Press, 1993).

Buber, M., *I and Thou* (Edinburgh: T&T Clark, 1958).

Capps, D., *The Depleted Self: Sin in a Narcissistic Age* (Minneapolis: Fortress Press, 1993).

Carmichael, K., *Sin and Forgiveness: New Responses in a Changing World* (Aldershot: Ashgate, 2003).

Ceccin, G., 'Address to Association for Family Therapy', *Context* 8.4.

Cobley, P., *Narrative* (London: Routledge, 2003).

Cotter, J., *Prayer in the Morning* (Exeter: Jim Cotter, 1987).

Coupland, D., *Life After God* (London: Simon & Schuster, 1995).

Crites, S., 'The Narrative Quality of Experience', in *Why Narrative? Readings in Narrative Theology* (ed.) S. Hauerwas and G.L. Jones (Grand Rapids: Eerdmans, 1989), 66-88.

Fackre, G., 'Narrative Theology: An Overview', *Interpretation* 37 (1983), 340–52.

Fletcher, J., 'Sin in Contemporary Literature', *Theology Today* 50.2 (1993), 254–64.

Fowler, J., *Faithful Change* (Nashville: Abingdon Press, 1996).

Frei, H.W., 'Theological Reflections on the Accounts of Jesus' Death and Resurrection', in *Hans Frei: Theology and Narrative: Selected Essays* (ed.) G. Hunsinger and W. Placher (Oxford: Oxford University Press, 1993), 45–93.

Gay, C.M., *The Way of the (Modern) World* (Grand Rapids: Eerdmans, 1998).

Gestrich, C., *The Return of Splendor in the World* (Grand Rapids: Eerdmans, 1997).

Giddens, A., *Modernity and Self Identity: Self and Society in the Late Modern Age* (Cambridge: Polity Press, 1991).

Goldberg, C., *Understanding Shame* (Northvale: Jason Aronson, 1991).

Goldingay, J., 'Old Testament Sacrifice and the Death of Christ', in *Atonement Today* (London: SPCK, 1995), 3–20.

—, *Models for Scripture* (Carlisle: Paternoster, 1987).

Good Will Hunting (London: Miramax Films and Buena Vista Home Entertainment, 1997).

Gorringe, T., *The Signs of Love: Reflections on the Eucharist* (London: SPCK, 1997).

Green, G., *Imagining God: Theology and the Religious Imagination* (Grand Rapids: Eerdmans, 1989).

Green, J.B., *The Gospel of Luke* (Grand Rapids: Eerdmans, 1997).

Green, J.B., and M.D. Baker, *Recovering the Scandal of the Cross* (Carlisle: Paternoster/Downers Grove: IVP, 2000).

Grenz, S., and R.E. Olson, *Twentieth-Century Theology* (Carlisle: Paternoster, 1992).

Grey, M., *Redeeming the Dream: Feminism, Redemption and Christian Tradition* (London: SPCK, 1989).

Gunton, C.E., *The Actuality of Atonement* (Edinburgh: T&T Clark, 1988).

Hall, D.J., *The Cross in Our Context* (Minneapolis: Fortress Press, 2003).

Hardy, B., 'Towards a Poetics of Fiction: An Approach through Narrative', *Novel* 2 (1968), 5–14.

Hughes, K.T., 'Framing Judas', *Semeia* 54 (1991), 223–31.

Humphrys, J., *Devil's Advocate* (London: Arrow Books, 2000).

Jensen, K.B., *The Social Semiotics of Mass Communication* (London: SAGE Publications, 1995).

Jones, G.L., *Embodying Forgiveness: A Theological Analysis* (Grand Rapids: Eerdmans, 1995).

Kaufman, G., *Shame: The Power of Caring* (Rochester: Shenkman Books, 1985).

Kaufman, G., and L. Raphael, *Coming Out of Shame: Transforming Gay and Lesbian Lives* (New York: Doubleday, 1996).

Kingsbury, J., *Matthew as Story* (Philadelphia: Fortress Press, 1988).

Klassen, W., *Judas: Betrayer or Friend of Jesus?* (London: SCM Press, 1996).

Kodell, J., *The Eucharist in the New Testament* (Wilmington: Glazier, 1988).

Lasch, C., *The Culture of Narcissism* (New York: W.W. Norton, 1991).

Leach, K., *The Sky is Red: Discerning the Signs of the Times* (London: Darton, Longman and Todd, 1997).

Levinas, E., and R. Kearney, 'Dialogue with Emmanuel Levinas', in *Face to Face with Levinas* (ed.) R.A. Cohen (Albany: State University of New York Press, 1986).

Long, T.G., 'God be Merciful to Me', *Theology Today* 50.2 (1993), 165–68.

Loughlin, G., *Telling God's Story: Bible, Church and Narrative Theology* (Cambridge: Cambridge University Press, 1996).

Lundin, R., *The Culture of Interpretation* (Grand Rapids: Eerdmans, 1993).

MacIntyre, A., *After Virtue* (Notre Dame: Notre Dame University Press, 1981).

McLeod, J., *Narrative and Psychotherapy* (London: SAGE Publications, 1997).

Meyer, B.F., *The Aims of Jesus* (London: SCM Press, 1979).

Middleton, J.R., and B.J. Walsh, *Truth Is Stranger than It Used to Be: Biblical Faith in a Postmodern Age* (London: SPCK, 1995).

Morgan, A., *What Is Narrative Therapy?* (Adelaide: Dulwich Centre Publications, 2000).

Parry, A., and R.E. Doan, *Story Re-Visions: Narrative Therapy in the Postmodern World* (New York: Guildford Press, 1994).

Pattison, S., *Shame: Theory, Therapy, Theology* (Cambridge: Cambridge University Press, 2000).

Patton, J., *Is Human Forgiveness Possible? A Pastoral Care Perspective* (Lima: Academic Renewal Press, 2003).

Payne, M., *Narrative Therapy* (London: SAGE Publications, 2000).

Pearse, M., *Why the Rest Hates the West: Understanding the Roots of Global Rage* (London: SPCK, 2003).

Rhoades, D., and D. Michie, *Mark as Story* (Philadelphia: Fortress Press, 1982).

Richards, S., 'Doing the Story: Narrative, Mission and Eucharist', in *Mass Culture: Eucharist and Mission in a Post-Modern World* (ed.) P. Ward (Oxford: Bible Reading Fellowship, 1999), 116–30.

Robinson, E., *The Language of Mystery* (London: SCM Press, 1987).

Root, M., 'The Narrative Structure of Soteriology', *Modern Theology* 2.2 (1986), 145–59.

Ruether, R.R., *Introducing Redemption in Christian Feminism* (Sheffield: Sheffield Academic Press, 1998).

Sankey, J., 'With, Through, and in Christ: A Eucharistic Approach to Atonement', in *Atonement Today* (ed.) J. Goldingay (London: SPCK, 1995), 93–110.

Senior, D., *The Passion of Jesus in the Gospel of Mark* (Wilmington: Glazier, 1984).

Sherry, P., *Images of Redemption* (London: T&T Clark, 2003).

Smith, D. E., and H.E. Taussig, *Many Tables: The Eucharist in the New Testament and Liturgy Today* (London: SCM Press, 1990).

Stroup, G.W., *The Promise of Narrative Theology* (London: SCM Press, 1984).

Sykes, S.W., 'Story and Eucharist', *Interpretation* 37 (1983), 365–76.

Tannehill, R.C., *Luke* (Nashville: Abingdon Press, 1996).

TeSelle, S., *Speaking in Parables* (London: SCM Press, 1975).

Thiselton, A.C., *Interpreting God and the Postmodern Self* (Edinburgh: T&T Clark, 1995).

Thorne, B., *Person-centred Counselling and Christian Spirituality: The Secular and the Holy* (London: Whurr Publishers, 2000).

Volf, M., *Exclusion and Embrace: A Theological Exploration of Identity, Otherness, and Reconciliation* (Nashville: Abingdon Press, 1996).

Walker, A., *Telling the Story* (London: SPCK, 1996).

Whelan, C.F., 'Suicide in the Ancient World: A Re-Examination of Matt 27:3–10', *Laval Théologique et Philosophique* 49 (1993), 505–22

Wilder, A., 'Story and Story-World', *Interpretation* 37 (1983) 353-64.

Williams, A.N., 'The Eucharist as Sacrament of Union', in *Sin, Death and the Devil* (ed.) C.E. Broaten and R.W. Jensen (Grand Rapids: Eerdmans, 2000), 45–75.

Williams, R., *Lost Icons: Reflections on Cultural Bereavement* (Edinburgh: T&T Clark, 2000).

Willomon, W.H., 'A Peculiarly Christian Account of Sin', *Theology Today* 50.2 (1993), 220–28.

Wilson, E.O., 'Wings across Two Cultures', *The Guardian: Saturday Review* (8 June 2000), 4.

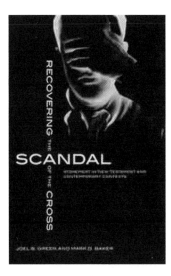

Recovering the Scandal of the Cross
The Atonement in New Testament and Contemporary Contexts

Joel Green and Mark Baker

Joel Green and Mark Baker provide an accessible introduction to the diverse theologies of the cross in the New Testament, down through the history of the church and on into the contemporary world. With three chapters on the cross in the New Testament, examinations of the main historical models of atonement and case studies in contemporary atonement theologies from Japan, Britain, Tanzania, the United States, as well as feminist theologies of the cross, *Recovering the Scandal of the Cross* shows readers how to think theologically for themselves in ways that are both creative and yet faithful to the inspired biblical testimony.

At the heart of this book is a challenge for us to view afresh the variety of contextual understandings of the death of Christ in the New Testament and to reconsider how we can faithfully communicate with fresh models the atoning significance of the cross for specific contexts today.

ISBN: 1-84227-246-2